BERLITZ®

BERLIN

By the staff of Berlitz Guides

HOW TO USE THIS GUIDE

- All the practical information, hints and tips that you will need before and during the trip start on page 99.

- For general background, see the sections Berlin and the Berliners, page 7, and A Brief History, page 13.

- The sights are described between pages 31 and 79.

   Our own choice of sights most highly recommended is pinpointed by the Berlitz traveller symbol.

- For hotel and restaurant recommendations, see the yellow pages in the centre of the guide.

- Nightlife, sports, shopping and festivals are recounted from pages 81 to 91, while information on restaurants and cuisine is to be found between pages 93 and 98.

- The maps are grouped on pages 121–126.

- If there's anything you can't find, refer to the index, pages 127–128.

Although we have made every effort to ensure the accuracy of all the information in this book, changes occur incessantly. We cannot therefore take responsibility for any facts, prices, addresses and circumstances in general that are constantly subject to alteration.

Text: Jack Altman
Staff Editor: Barbara Ender
Design, layout and photography: Dominique Michellod
Additional photos: cover, pp. 40, 60, 80, 85 Claude Huber; pp. 2–3, 78–79 VISUM/Michael Lange; p. 24 PRISMA/Etienne; p. 41 PRISMA/Earl of Winden; p. 56 VISUM/Rudi Meisel; p. 89 VISUM/Gerd Ludwig; p. 96 Stephan Schraps.
Cartography: 𝐹𝑎𝑙𝑘 Falk Verlag, Hamburg

We would like to thank Richard Campbell and Sarah Fleming for their invaluable help in the preparation of this guide.

CONTENTS

BERLIN AND THE BERLINERS

Is there a city on earth more evocative of modern European history than Berlin? In the 120 years since it first became Germany's capital, it has excited pride for its strength, admiration for its culture, hatred as the centre of Hitler's tyranny, compassion as a bastion of post-war freedom, and fear as a focus of Cold War conflict. More than any other capital, Berlin symbolizes the immense changes wrought in eastern and western Europe as the century draws to a close.

But it is also a city of enthusiasm and fun. If Germany has a sense of humour, its headquarters is Berlin.

For each emotion which the name Berlin evokes, the city has appropriate symbols. The

As the modern city confidently faces the future, the ruin of Kaiser Wilhelm Memorial Church recalls World War II.

noble Charlottenburg palace and royal monuments on Unter den Linden honour the formidable Prussian past, while the Brandenburg Gate proclaims the city's regained unity.

The Kurfürstendamm was long a defiant showcase of the western prosperity supporting West Berlin when it was isolated. The boulevard can now relinquish its function of commercial propaganda and merely reflect the ebullience of the 1920s, at once elegant and garish.

The Reichstag recalls united Germany's attempts at parliamentary democracy, while the gigantic Olympic Stadium expresses the bombast of Hitler's dictatorship. The chaos and destruction he wreaked have a quite deliberate reminder in the bombed-out shell of the Kaiser Wilhelm Memorial Church. And here and there, like relics of some medieval fortification, you can still come across remains of the Wall that divided the city, enough to conjure up all the chilling confrontations of East and West.

Relics of the East-West Divide

The city's eastern districts—Mitte, Prenzlauer Berg, Pankow and Friedrichshain—form essentially the old, densely populated centre whose tenements (disparagingly referred to as *Mietskasernen*, literally "rental barracks") inspired the 1920s proletarian theatre of Erwin Piscator and Bertolt Brecht. When post-war Berlin was divided, it was appropriate that the Soviet sector devoted to the Communist experiment should cover most of the working-class neighbourhoods, while West Berlin had as its centre the eminently bourgeois neighbourhood of Charlottenburg.

Today, even with the Wall dismantled, a division of 45 years has left the city in two visually distinct halves. It will take some time and a huge ongoing investment for, in Willy Brandt's now immortal words, "what belongs together to grow together". But for all the dilapidation that much of eastern Berlin has suffered, many of its neighbourhoods still give a more authentic idea of what the city was like in the 1920s and 30s. West Berliners in 1945 had been happy to break with their past and opt, by and large, for a new, Americanized city. The city's eastern sector, on the other hand, was less subject to the Russian model of Stalinistic architecture and, largely for lack of funds for new construction, held on to what remained of the old Berlin. A major attempt at modernity is apparent in the big Swedish-built hotels and monolithic official buildings on what was the ideological showplace of the Communists, between Marx-Engels-Platz and Alexanderplatz.

Breathing Space

Despite the stone, steel and glass, Berlin is the greenest metropolis in Europe. If a city had to be walled off from its hinterland, few were geographically better suited for survival than West Berlin when it came to breathing space. Fully one-third of its area consists of parkland and woods, lakes and rivers. Besides the Tiergarten and Spree river in the city centre, the south-west suburbs have the forest of Grunewald, the Havel river and the Wannsee, and in the north there's the Tegel forest and lake. Small garden colonies abound, even some flourishing little farming communities like Lübars inside the city limits. To all this, eastern Berlin now adds its own lake, the Grosser Müggelsee, and woods and parkland around Treptow and Köpenick.

And the hinterland itself is accessible again for delightful excursions. Potsdam, on the other side of the Glienicke Bridge, is within easy reach for a visit to Frederick the Great's Sanssouci Palace. Go boating on the Templiner lake, or rambling in the surrounding forests and parks of Charlottenhof, Petzow and Werder. Or make a pilgrimage to the Cistercian monastery of Lehnin near the town of Brandenburg.

Optimistic Future

Boosted by the fall of the Wall, the city is more vibrant and forward-looking than ever in its artistic, intellectual and economic activities.

The Cultural Forum in the Tiergarten is expanding its concert halls and art galleries. Ambitious plans are proceeding to restore the magnificent Museum Island in the middle of the Spree river. The city has three major symphony orchestras, and three opera and comic opera houses. Western Berlin's Schiller Theatre and Schau-bühne form with the Berliner Ensemble and Deutsches Theater in the east one of the world's most formidable theatre establishments. Typical of Berlin itself, this establishment promotes both classical tradition and the avant-garde.

Cinema, with the Berlin Film Festival as its flagship, is resuming the activity of its great creative period in the 1920s. German producers are uniting with international film companies to redevelop Berlin's own "Hollywood", the Babelsberg studios, attached to Potsdam just outside the capital.

Well over 100,000 students, professors and other academic personnel work in a buoyant atmosphere in the three universities and numerous research institutes. Adding to the considerable investment in textiles, chemicals, engineering and electrical equipment, many more big companies—German, Japanese and American—have set up new operations to cash in on the city's future.

Young at Heart

Beyond the sightseeing, the most fascinating thing about Berlin is the people. Throughout the city's turbulent history, one constant has forced the admiration of the often-perplexed watching world: the individualism, courage and wit of the Berliners themselves. A preconceived notion of Germans as a whole, but particularly of Prussians, has often presented them as a people cool and unfeeling. Such notions were refuted by the sight of the Berliners' flood of simple warm emotion and good humour when the Wall was breached on November 9, 1989.

The town holds on to its old customs but remains very young at heart. During the years of the Cold War, a disproportionately elderly population was rejuvenated by the influx of students and artists, encouraged by special government subsidies and exemption from military service.

Younger Berlin's so-called alternative scene has revived the city's 1920s reputation of lively and wildly independent-minded creativity—sometimes foundering in disillusioned nihilism in its strongholds, the working-class districts of Kreuzberg and Neukölln.

The Berliners live in usually convivial anarchy with a large contingent of *Gastarbeiter* or "guest-workers", coming principally from Turkey. Resisting the xenophobic assaults of the lunatic fringe of local right-wing extremists, the Turks and other Mediterraneans have added considerable colour and more varied gastronomy to Berlin's social life. The spirit is typified by their animated market on the Maibachufer of the Landwehr canal.

Some fear that the town's renewed status as the capital of a united Germany will make the people more bourgeois, more "establishment", more materialistic. Certainly, the Porsches, BMWs and Mercedes are on the increase, shiny new bars for the modish night people are mushrooming around the Tiergarten and Potsdamer Strasse, and some of the old working-class neighbourhoods in eastern and western Berlin are being renovated and pushed into higher rent brackets. But Berlin has always been big enough to house both the smart and the tawdry, the authentic and the fake, the traditional sand the avant-garde. The town is getting ready for the 21st century. Come and watch.

With the German flag flying on the Reichstag behind her, the lady touts the charms of Berlin— like her, big and breezy.

A BRIEF HISTORY

Now that it is back in one piece, the German capital can recall with a smile that it became a municipality in the 1200s as a divided city. In those days the two rival halves were in no great hurry to unite. The fishermen of Cölln, whose name survives in the modern borough of Neukölln, lived on an island in the Spree river, joined to the mainland by what is now the Mühlendamm embankment. On the north bank lived the carters and innkeepers of Berlin. The townships that comprise the modern Mitte district grew up around market places over which their churches, the Nikolaikirche and Marienkirche, still tower today. With the fortress of Burg Köpenick providing a common defence to the south, Cölln and Berlin together formed an important

One of Berlin's leading banks rises gleaming above the symbolic rubble of the past.

trade centre on the route between Magdeburg and Poznan.

In a region inhabited by the Slavonic Sorbs, the city's population was overwhelmingly German by the 13th century—enterprising merchants from the northern Rhineland, Westphalia and Lower Saxony with latecomers from the Harz and Thuringia. Berlin and Cölln united in 1307 to lead the Brandenburg region's defences against robber barons who were terrorizing merchants and local peasants. The prosperous city became a member of the Hanseatic League, trading in rye, wool and oak timber and providing an entrepôt for skins and furs from eastern Europe. Living was apparently easy in the 15th century, as historian Trithemius noted: "Life here consists of nothing but eating and drinking." Nothing fancy, just good solid fare—meat or fish, lentils, groats and beer.

Berlin remained a virtually autonomous outpost of the

German empire until 1448, when Brandenburg's Kurfürst (Prince Elector) Friedrich II took over control of the city after crushing the citizens' violent resistance, the *Berliner Unwillen*. He was a member of the Hohenzollern dynasty that was to hold sway here for over 450 years.

The independent spirit of the Berliners made itself felt during the Reformation in the 16th century. The people were tired of paying the tribute exacted by the Catholic church. At a time when the citizens of other German principalities had to observe the religion of their prince, Berliners pressured Prince Elector Joachim II in 1539 to accept the Protestant creed as preached by Martin Luther. Symbolic of the new humanism and budding capitalism, the Franciscans' monastery was converted into a printing plant and publishing house, next door to the town's first school (Gymnasium) to be founded independently of the church.

Like the rest of Germany, the city was devastated by the Thirty Years' War (1618–48). Its Brandenburg rulers tried to befriend both the Protestant and Catholic armies and made enemies of both, leaving Berlin—unfortified—to pay the price.

Enter Prussia—and Napoleon

With his vision of uniting Brandenburg and Prussia in one state, it was the Great Elector Friedrich Wilhelm (1640–88) who prepared Berlin to become a strong capital, immediately fortifying it as a garrison town. But the urgency of replenishing its depleted population with new stock gave it a cosmopolitan flavour that set it apart from other German cities. The first newcomers were 50 wealthy Jewish families expelled from Vienna in 1671. They were followed 14 years later by 5,600 Huguenot Protestants driven out of France by the revocation of the Edict of Nantes. At a time when France was Europe's cultural master, these sophisticated merchants and highly skilled craftsmen—jewellers, tailors, pastry chefs and restaurant-owners—brought a new refinement to the town.

This was enhanced by the advent of the Great Elector's son who in 1701 crowned himself in Königsberg (now Kaliningrad) King Friedrich I *in* (not *of*) Prussia. (Part of the country remained in Polish hands.) Prompted by his energetic and cultivated wife Sophie Charlotte, the king founded academies in Berlin for the arts and sciences, the latter with philosopher Gottfried Leibniz as its president. Baroque master Andreas Schlüter was commissioned to redesign the royal palace. It was destroyed in 1951 to make way for East Germany's Palast der Republik on what is now Marx-Engels-Platz, but Sophie Charlotte's grand residence, Schloss Charlottenburg, has survived as a model of the era's elegance and grace.

Despising the Baroque glitter of his parents' court, Friedrich Wilhelm I (1713–40) subjected the hitherto easy-going Berliners to a frugal, rigid concept of *Preussentum* (Prussianness): unquestioning obedience to the ruler and his administrators, and sharply defined class distinctions affirming the supremacy of the aristocracy and officer class and that of soldiers over civilians in general.

Friedrich der Grosse (Frederick the Great, 1740–86), king *of* and not just *in* Prussia, took his realm to the forefront of European politics and had little time for Berlin. He concentrated on turning his beloved Potsdam into a mini-Versailles where French was spoken and Voltaire became his philosopher-in-residence. He rarely appeared in Berlin except to garner public support—and taxes—after his return from costly wars with the Silesians, Russians and Austrians. But he

A KING AND CABBAGES

An English cousin referred to Friedrich Wilhelm I as "my brother the Sergeant", and the nickname stuck. The Sergeant King spent his life in uniform and his courtiers followed suit. He had two obsessions: corporal punishment for the troops and washing his hands wherever he went. Irascible and deeply religious, he was simple in his personal tastes, finding his pleasure in strictly male company over a pipe of tobacco and tankard of beer—wine struck him as too expensive. When he came to the throne, a wag's graffiti on the palace wall pinpointed the costs of his parents' extravagance: "This castle is for rent and the royal residence of Berlin for sale." To pay off the debts, he cut court officials' salaries from 250,000 silver thalers to 50,000, sold the opulent coronation robes, melted down the palace silver, tore the flowers out of the Charlottenburg palace gardens and replaced them with cabbages.

did leave the capital an enduring legacy with the monumental Forum Fridericianum laid out on Unter den Linden by his architect Georg von Knobelsdorff (see p. 44). He also promoted the manufacture of silk and velvet, set up local banks to make the city independent of the Hanseatic towns, and opened a royal porcelain factory still operating today.

The armies of Frederick's successors proved no match for Napoleon's Grande Armée. As the French advanced through eastern Germany in 1806 with victories at Jena and Auerstedt, the Berlin beaurocracy, bourgeoisie and court fled to their country estates along the Oder river. No troops were left to defend the city. Napoleon's march into Berlin through the Brandenburg Gate kindled the flame of German patriotism.

Capital of Germany

Defying the two-year French occupation, philosopher Johann Gottlieb Fichte exhorted the German people to assume their destiny as a nation. Drummers in French parades on Unter den Linden were ordered to drown out his fiery Sunday speeches at the Royal Academy.

One of the uniting forces for the nationalist movement after the defeat of Napoleon was the innovation in Berlin of mass open-air gymnastics—until the Prussian authorities suppressed the communal knee-bends and scissor-jumps as subversive. Potentially more dangerous were the *Lesecafés* (reading cafés) such as Spargnapani and Kranzler—the latter still going strong but less subversive now. They were a rendezvous for the intelligentsia who met to read foreign and provincial newspapers for information withheld in the heavily censored Berlin press. Working men talked politics in beer gardens such as Die Zelte in the Tiergarten.

The accelerating industrial revolution had produced a new Berlin proletariat of 50,000 workers crammed into the infamous tenement buildings known as *Mietskasernen* ("rental barracks"). In the wake of the 1848 revolts in Paris and Vienna, demonstrations protesting at working and living conditions in Berlin were crushed by the Prussian cavalry, leaving 230 dead. The king made small concessions, paying lip service

The imperial German eagle still emblazons a gate at Charlottenburg Palace.

to popular demand for freedom of the press and a constitutional rather than absolutist monarchy. But a year later police controls were tightened, press censorship resumed and democratic meetings were swarming with government spies.

Prussia's success in the Franco-Prussian War (1870–71) placed it at the head of a new united Germany. Under Kaiser Wilhelm I and Otto von Bismarck, known as the Iron Chancellor, Berlin became the *Reichshauptstadt* (capital of the empire). By 1880, amid the industrial expansion of the *Gründerzeit* (founding years), the city's population soared past the million mark. Berlin boomed as the centre of the country's machine industry. It was a perfect market for mass-circulation newspapers and big department stores such as KaDeWe, the Kaufhaus des Westens, that would one day symbolize consumer heaven for "liberated" East Germans.

After that emphatically philistine period of rapid growth, the city at last began to take its place as Germany's cultural as well as political capital. Berlin artists Max Liebermann, Lovis Corinth and Max Slevogt challenged Munich's dominance of German painting. The Phil-

harmonic asserted an international prestige, attracting Tchaikovsky, Grieg and Strauss as guest composers. In 1905, the great Viennese director Max Reinhardt arrived to head the Deutsches Theater and make Berlin Europe's leading theatre city.

Among its scientists, Robert Koch won a Nobel prize for his discovery of the tuberculosis bacillus, physicist Max Planck headed the new Kaiser Wilhelm Society for the Advancement of Science (later named the Max-Planck-Institut), with Albert Einstein as director of the physics department. It was said that of the ten people who understood Einstein's theory of relativity at that time, eight were living in Berlin.

War and Revolution

After years of opposition on the social front, Berliners solidly supported what proved to be the Hohenzollerns' last military gasp—World War I. At the start of hostilities in August 1914, people gathered in thousands to cheer the Kaiser and his wife at the royal palace. But enthusiasm was short-lived.

Food shortages—turnips had replaced the sacred German potato—and horrendous loss of life on the front turned popular feeling against the war. In 1916, Karl Liebknecht and Rosa Luxemburg formed the Spartacus League, precursor of the German Communist Party. Two years later, with Germany defeated and insurrections in Kiel, Munich, Hamburg and Stuttgart, revolution broke out in Berlin. Truckloads of fraternizing soldiers and workers rode together through the streets, armed with machine guns and waving the red flag. As the Social Democrats were proclaiming a new German Republic, Liebknecht took over the royal palace and declared the republic socialist, with "supreme authority for the workers and soldiers".

Vehemently opposed to any Soviet-style revolution, Chancellor Friedrich Ebert and his Social Democrats outmanoeuvred the Spartacists. Ruthless defence minister Gustav Noske called in 4,000 *Freikorps* (rightwing storm-troopers) to smash the movement. They assassinated Liebknecht and Luxemburg on January 15, 1919. (A plaque on the Lützowufer marks the spot where Rosa Luxemburg's body was fished out of the Landwehr canal.) Four days later, a new National Assembly was elected and the dominant Social Democrats

moved the government to the safety of Weimar, some 150 miles south-west of Berlin, to draw up the constitution of the new republic.

The Crazy Twenties

The use of the Freikorps to suppress the Spartacists was to haunt the Weimar Republic. In March 1920, the Kapp Putsch brought 5,000 storm-troopers into Berlin. Wolfgang Kapp, an obscure civil servant, was installed as puppet chancellor. The coup lasted only five days, but it set the tone for Germany's fragile experiment in parliamentary democracy. The swastikas on Freikorps helmets reappeared on the armbands of Hitler's storm-troopers, who crushed all democracy in 1933.

The turbulent 20s gave Berlin a place apart in the world's popular imagination. In 1920, the incorporation of 8 townships and some 60 suburban communities into the metropolis doubled Berlin's population overnight to 4 million. Before democracy died in 1933, the city experienced a charmed life of exciting and disturbing creativity that left its stamp on the whole of European culture. Defeat in World War I had shattered the rigid certainties of Berlin's "Prussianness" and left the town open to radical, often wildly eccentric ideas—adventures in social and artistic expression almost unimaginable in the older cultural capitals of Vienna, London and Paris.

Artists of the avant-garde Dada movement called for state prayers to be replaced by simultaneous poetry, for progressive unemployment by immediate mechanization of all physical labour, and for regulation of sexual intercourse through a Central Dada Sex Office. Long before the New York "happenings" of the 1960s, Berlin Dadaists organized races between a sewing machine and a typewriter, with writer Walter Mehring and artist George Grosz as jockeys.

The hilariously absurd and the deadly serious went hand in hand. Nightclubs on Tauentzienstrasse combined striptease and fierce political satire. Heavy drinking, hashish and sexual licence accompanied acute analysis of the world scene. The painting of George Grosz, Otto Dix and Max Beckmann was brutally realist. Max Reinhardt's spectacular productions, theatrical equivalents of Hollywood film extravaganzas, yielded to the politically committed revolutionary theatre of Bertolt Brecht and Erwin Pisca-

tor, sharpened by Kurt Weill's acerbic music.

The dissonance of the times was aptly symbolized by the atonal music composed in Berlin by Arnold Schönberg and his pupil Alban Berg. Such was the creativity of this period that Berlin hosted the first performances of no less than 12 new operas from 1919 to 1932, with Erich Kleibe and Otto Klemperer as conductors. Wilhelm Furtwängler directed the Berlin Philharmonic and Bruno Walter the Städtische Oper.

The conservative establishment winced as the Prussian Writers' Academy chose as its president Heinrich Mann, the elder brother of Thomas Mann, a violent critic of the German bourgeoisie and supporter of the Communist Party. His best-known novel, *Professor Unrat,* inspired Josef von Sternberg's *The Blue Angel,* the film that revealed the vocal talents (and thighs) of Marlene Dietrich.

Berlin showed its sense of the times with its mastery of film, the 20th-century art form. Fritz Lang, F.W. Murnau,

On horseback in the courtyard of Schloss Charlottenburg: Prussia's Great Elector, Friedrich Wilhelm.

G.W. Pabst and Ernst Lubitsch were the leading directors of their generation. Whereas Hollywood had understood cinema as an industry of mass entertainment, Berlin film makers added a new perception of its artistic possibilities with *M, Caligari, Nosferatu* and *Lulu*. After seeing *Metropolis,* Lang's premonitory fable of human regimentation, Hitler wanted the master of dark spectacle to make films for him.

Berlin was going through a wild time of bread and circuses, but the bread was proving enormously expensive and the circus was bloody. At the start of the 20s, inflation had made nonsense of Germany's currency: people went shopping with suitcases full of money. Political assassination became routine, the most significant victim being foreign minister Walther Rathenau, an enlightened democrat and Jew killed near the Grunewald forest. Berlin was the scene of vicious street battles between Communist and Nazi factions exploiting the social disruptions of inflation and unemployment.

The Third Reich

Communist hostility to the Social Democrats split the opposition to the Nazis. Hitler became chancellor on January 30, 1933. A month later, the Reichstag building went up in flames. A Dutch Communist, Marinus van der Lubbe, was arrested on the spot. He confessed to the crime, insisting he had acted alone. Although it was never explained how one man with only his shirt for tinder could have set the whole building alight three minutes after he entered it, no conclusive proof has been offered for either a Nazi or German Communist plot. But Hitler used the fire as a pretext to eliminate Communist and all left-wing opposition from German political life. The Nazi reign of terror had begun.

Flames were the leitmotiv of the Third Reich in Berlin. On May 10, 1933, a torchlight procession brought thousands of students—the Nazis had intellectual thugs, too—along Unter den Linden to the square in front of the university. They carried books, not to a lecture but to a bonfire on which were burned the works of Thomas Mann, Heinrich Mann, Stefan Zweig, Albert Einstein and Sigmund Freud, as well as Proust, Zola, Gide, H.G. Wells, Upton Sinclair and Jack London.

In 1936 a flame was brought from Athens to Berlin to inaugurate the Olympic Games, a personal triumph for Hitler. In deference to foreign visitors, anti-Semitic signs such as *Juden unerwünscht* (Jews undesirable) were removed from shops, hotels and cafés. As soon as the foreigners had left town, the signs went up again. Discrimination against Jews moved inexorably to the night of November 9, 1938, when flames rose over Berlin as synagogues and other Jewish-owned buildings were burned to the ground. Amid the smashed glass of the looted shops, Berliners' wit eased their discomfort by referring to the event as *Kristallnacht* (Crystal Night). The city's Jewish population, 160,564 in 1933, was reduced by emigration and extermination to 7,272 in 1945. With the creation of the state of Israel, the community continued to dwindle to a few hundred, but with recent immigration from the Soviet Union it has begun to grow again.

World War II

In the autumn of 1938, Hitler was upset that Berliners did not share his enthusiasm for the cavalcade of troops driving along Wilhelmstrasse. The army was preparing its march into Czechoslovakia, but onlookers showed none of the fervour that had greeted military parades in 1914.

Their disquiet was soon to be justified by the rain of bombs on the capital, wreaking destruction that represented one-seventh of Germany's total war damage. The first attacks came in 1940 from the British in retaliation for the London Blitz. Raids were stepped up after the German debacle of Stalingrad in 1943, with mass Anglo-American "carpet bombing". The worst single raid came on February 6, 1945, when bombs wiped out 4 sq. km. (1½ sq. mi.) of the city centre in one hour.

Hitler spent the last days of the war in his bunker at the Reich chancellery. As Soviet troops moved in to capture the city, Hitler killed himself with a shot through the mouth.

The war ended with unconditional German surrender on May 7, 1945. In Berlin, the people were left to pick up the pieces—literally. Women organized themselves into groups of *Trümmerfrauen* (rubble women), 60,000 of them passing the debris of war from hand to hand to clear ground for rebuilding. Eventually there was sufficient rubble to create a few artificial mountains. One of them, Teufelsberg in the Grunewald, is big enough for skiing.

The City Divided

With the Soviet army already in place, American troops entered Berlin on their Independence Day, July 4, followed by British and French contingents. Four-power control of Berlin was formalized at Potsdam by Winston Churchill (replaced in mid-conference by Clement Attlee, his successor as prime minister), Harry Truman and Joseph Stalin. The Soviet eastern sector covered just under half the city's area. The western sector was divided among the French in the north around Tegel Airport, the British largely in the centre from the Tiergarten to Spandau, and the Americans in the sprawling south-west corner from Kreuzberg out to the Grunewald and Wannsee.

The administrative divisions soon became hard political realities as the Western Allies found themselves confronted with Soviet efforts to incorporate the whole of Berlin into a new communist-controlled German Democratic Republic.

Mallet and chisel replaced hammer and sickle as people feverishly hacked away at the hated Berlin Wall.

In the 1946 municipal elections—Berlin's first free vote since 1933 and its last as a united city until 1990—the Social Democrats won a crushing victory over the Communists, prompting the Soviets to tighten their grip on the eastern sector. Understandably unhappy that West Berlin's capitalist presence in the middle of East Germany was having a subversive influence on the Communist experiment, the Soviets and their East German allies began to restrict traffic from West Germany. In June 1948, road, rail and waterway routes to West Berlin were sealed off. From bases in Frankfurt, Hamburg and Hanover, the Western Allies countered the blockade by airlifting into Berlin between 4,000 and 8,000 tons of food and other vital supplies every day for 11 months. The blockade ended in May 1949, and West Berlin became a *Land* linked administratively with, but not yet politically incorporated into, the new Federal Republic of Germany. East Berlin was proclaimed capital of the fledgling German Democratic Republic.

Discontent with conditions in East Berlin first erupted into open revolt on June 17, 1953. Construction workers on strike marched down Stalinallee (at present Karl-Marx-Allee) and led violent demonstrations against the government of Walter Ulbricht. They protested the state demands for increased productivity while their living standards continued to compare unfavourably with West Berlin's. The uprising was crushed by Soviet tanks.

By the end of the 1950s the flow of refugees to the West had reached disastrous proportions for East Germany. More than 3 million citizens had fled, over half of them through Berlin where border controls were only perfunctory. When Khrushchev decided to stop the haemorrhage, the country was losing millions of marks invested in the training of doctors, engineers and other highly skilled workers seeking better wages in the West.

In the early hours of August 13, 1961, East German workers and soldiers began erecting the Wall that would separate East and West Berlin and change the lives of several million people for nearly 30 years. It began with barbed wire and road blocks. Refugees continued to make their way through the new barriers, swimming through sewers and canals, jumping from buildings and railway bridges overlooking West Berlin. Soon huge slabs of reinforced concrete and tank-traps formed a more lasting and impenetrable barrier (see p. 48). Crossing points were established for foreigners and for West Germans, but not for Berliners until a tiny few were allowed across much later in the Cold War confrontation.

For the western alliance, the Wall made West Berlin an even more powerful propaganda symbol of democratic freedom. On his visit in 1963, President John F. Kennedy dramatically underlined the Western Allies' commitment to the city, with his proclamation: *"Ich bin ein Berliner."*

The City Reunited

The Wall did halt the flow of refugees to a few isolated escapes by tunnel or other ingenious subterfuges, but the East German economy suffered from the more devastating assaults of massive mismanagement and high-level corruption. Erich Honecker's regime won international diplomatic recognition

Rebuilding the dilapidated eastern part of the city is a big headache, despite the odd showplace skyscraper.

for East Berlin as its capital and, with gleaming Scandinavian-built hotels and other skyscrapers, tried to give it a lustre to rival that of West Berlin. But beneath the surface, the essential mediocrity of daily life and lack of personal freedom continued to undermine any chance of popular support.

Dissident intellectuals were expelled. Art remained stultifyingly official. In 1987, a western rock concert near the Wall loudly amplified eastwards attracted East Berlin youths who chanted: "The Wall must fall! The Wall must fall!"

But the final impetus for its collapse came from the provinces, when an ecological campaign in Leipzig against industrial pollution and nuclear weapons grew into nationwide pressure for democratic freedom. In 1989, with thousands of East Germans fleeing to the West via Hungary, Czechoslovakia and Poland, the country was swept up in the wave of eastern European revolutions unleashed by the reforms of Mikhail Gorbachov. His visit to East Berlin for the German Democratic Republic's 40th anniversary in October left it clear that Soviet troops would no longer support its moribund regime. On November 9, 1989,

the Berlin Wall was opened. Some 11 months later, the stroke of midnight heralding the day of national unity, October 3, 1990, Berlin's church bells rang out and a huge black, red and gold national flag was hoisted at the Reichstag. East and West Berlin were again one city.

With a population in June 1990 of 3,418,135, Berlin was far and away Germany's largest city and quickly declared the national capital again. International businessmen and bankers flocked into town, but Bonn, understandably, and many provincial politicians opposing too great a concentration of power in Berlin, were reluctant to see all the affairs of government desert the banks of the Rhine. With autonomy-conscious *Länder* fearing the centralization that had undermined German democracy in the past, the transfer of political power promised to be a delicate and gradual process. Turning its back on its left-wing tradition, the city elected in 1990 a conservative mayor to cope with the enormous day-to-day problems in housing, employment and traffic congestion arising from reunification. Whatever happens, Berlin's role is assured as the exciting star at centre stage of German life.

HISTORICAL LANDMARKS

Beginnings
1237–44	First record of Cölln and Berlin.
1307	Two townships united as one city.
1359	Berlin joins Hanseatic League.
1448	Friedrich II asserts rule of Hohenzollern dynasty.

Reformation
1539	Berliners force Joachim II to turn Protestant.
1618–48	War and plague cut population in half to barely 5,000.
1671–85	Jews and Huguenots add cosmopolitan flavour.
1696–1700	Arts and science academies founded.

Rise of Prussia
1740–86	Frederick the Great gives Unter den Linden its major monuments.
1791	Brandenburg Gate completed.
1806–08	Napoleon occupies Berlin.
1810	Humboldt founds University.
1838	City's first railway, to Potsdam.
1848	Democratic revolt crushed.

Capital of Germany
1871	Bismarck imposes Berlin as capital of German Reich.
1918	New republic declared at Reichstag.
1920	Metropolis of 4 million after suburbs annexed.
1933	Hitler imposes dictatorship after Reichstag fire.
1936	Berlin hosts Olympic Games.
1938	Jewish-owned buildings destroyed in *Kristallnacht* pogrom.
1939–45	World War II reduces population from 4,300,000 to 2,800,000.

Towards Unity
1948–49	Western airlift breaks Soviet blockade of West Berlin.
1953	Soviet tanks crush East Berlin uprising.
1961	Wall built to stem flow of refugees to West Berlin.
1989	East German regime toppled, Wall opened November 9.
1990	Reunited German capital, population 3,418,135, elects conservative mayor.

WHAT TO SEE

Careful planning is needed for a thorough visit of Berlin—with a total area of 883 sq. km. (340 sq. mi.) it is more than eight times the size of Paris. Since the municipal transport system was reorganized to serve the whole city, much can be visited with the excellent underground *(U-Bahn)* and overhead *(S-Bahn)* railways or the delightful double-decker buses. But we recommend renting a car to reach conveniently the outlying areas, especially the museums in Dahlem and the recreation parks and lakes in the Grunewald and out at the Müggelsee.

To get your bearings, start with an organized sightseeing tour—by bus, for instance, departing from the east end of the Kurfürstendamm. Cruises on the Spree and Havel rivers and the Landwehr canal offer a more leisurely way of taking in areas of eastern and western Berlin that are not normally covered by the tour buses. The monuments seen from a duck's-eye view make original photographs.

In the past, visits were inevitably split into two, west and then east, and indeed, despite

THE ESSENTIALS

For those on a brief visit to Berlin or who want to see the main sights before making a more thorough tour of the town, here are the principal highlights, in no order of priority:

Kurfürstendamm
Reichstag
Brandenburg Gate
Unter den Linden
Schloss Charlottenburg
Grunewald
Ägyptisches Museum
Pergamon Museum
Gemäldegalerie, Dahlem
Neue Nationalgalerie

Nightlife around the Ku'damm makes Berlin one of the most exciting towns in Europe.

the disappearance of the Wall, there is still a palpable sense of crossing from one part of the city to the other. The division has left its scars. Sooner or later, however, talk of western or eastern Berlin will carry no more ideological ballast than New York's East Side and West Side or London's East End and West End. Already, although our itineraries take the old division into account, they crisscross the city from west to east and back again to give you a better sense of Berlin as a unified whole. For the sake of convenience, with its information centres and other well-organized tourist facilities, the area on and around the Kurfürstendamm is the best place to begin.

Around Kurfürstendamm

Berlin's main thoroughfare, literally "Prince Elector's Embankment", is known more simply to Berliners as the **Ku'damm**. It runs through the centre of the City, a roughly triangular precinct bounded by Leibnizstrasse, Hardenbergstrasse, Tauentzienstrasse and Lietzenburger Strasse. Here are most of the major shops, restaurants, cafés, cinemas, theatres and art galleries. You will find that racy combination of elegance, prosperity and cheerful impudence that has always distinguished Berlin from other German cities.

Reunification may begin to shift some of the emphasis of city life to the east as shops start opening new branches on Unter den Linden and Alexanderplatz, but the Ku'damm remains Germany's liveliest avenue, pulsating with traffic late into the night. Impressed by the prolongation of the Champs-Elysées in Paris to the Bois de Boulogne, Bismarck wanted to extend the Ku'damm out to the Grunewald forest. But the imperial pretensions were never realized, and ultimately the avenue linked Kaiser Wilhelm Memorial Church to nothing grander than the Halensee railway station.

Sooner or later, everyone comes to promenade on the Ku'damm, and a venerable place to watch them is the **Café Kranzler**, a veritable Berlin institution at the corner of Joachimstaler Strasse. It's decidedly bourgeois now, though the original Kranzler in the east was a hotbed of radical intellectuals in 1848 (see p. 16).

The avenue lost almost all the Jugendstil architecture of its Wilhelminian heyday in

World War II, but a vestige can be seen in the elegant **Café Möhring** across the road (next to Wertheim department store). Note, too, the façade of No. 52, a handsome Art Deco apartment building. Otherwise the street is resolutely modern—gleaming glass, steel and an occasional touch of marble—but still a magnet for fashionable shopping.

Off the avenue at Fasanenstrasse 79 is the **Jüdisches Gemeindezentrum** (Jewish Community Centre). Framing the entrance is the domed portal from the synagogue burned down in the fateful Kristallnacht of 1938 (see p. 23). The modern building serves as a cultural centre for the couple of thousand Jews still living in Berlin—there were 160,000 in 1933, one-third of all Jews in Germany. (Pending completion of the new building as part of the Berlin Museum in the Kreuzberg district, a Jewish Museum is housed in the Martin-Gropius-Bau, see p. 42.)

Take Kantstrasse to fashionable **Savignyplatz**, centre of some first-class art bookshops and galleries, outdoor cafés, bistrots and bars, particularly along Grolmanstrasse.

Back on the Ku'damm, head east to **Breitscheidplatz**. This is a popular gathering place to watch street theatre around Joachim Schmettau's granite **Weltkugelbrunnen** (Fountain of the World, 1983). The split globe symbolized the East-West division of which Berlin was

FINDING YOUR WAY...

Here are some common terms you may come across on road-signs and maps in Berlin:

Allee	boulevard
Bahnhof	railway station
Brücke	bridge
Brunnen	fountain
Burg	castle, fortress
Damm	embankment
Dom	cathedral
Forst	forest
Friedhof	cemetery
Gasse	alley, street
Insel	island
Kirche	church
Markt	market
Palast	palace
Palais	palace
Pfad	path
Rathaus	town hall
Schloss	castle, palace
See	lake
Strasse	street
Turm	tower
Ufer	river bank
Viertel	district, quarter
Wald	wood, forest
Weg	way

the centre. Soaring above it is another pregnant symbol, the **Kaiser-Wilhelm-Gedächtniskirche** (Kaiser Wilhelm Memorial Church). Bombs in 1943 and artillery fire at the end of the war left the tower with the broken stump of its spire—63 m. (206 ft.) high compared with the original 113 m.

(370 ft.)—as a monumental ruin to recall the city's destruction. Flanking it, a modern octagonal church to the east and a chapel and hexagonal tower to the west represent the city's postwar rebirth. Stained glass from Chartres set in walls of moulded concrete glows over the Ku'damm at night.

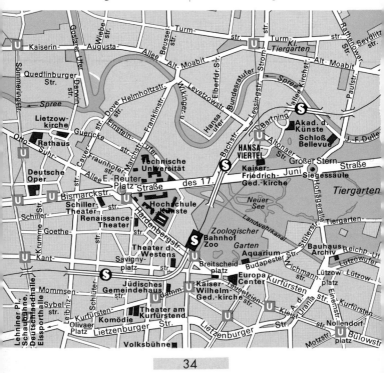

The remains of the neo-Romanesque church built to honour Wilhelm I constitute a memorial hall to celebrate the Hohenzollerns' pious monarchism. A mosaic of Christ the King is set above friezes and reliefs of Prussian monarchs from Prince Elector Friedrich I (1415–40) to the last crown prince, Friedrich Wilhelm, who died in 1951. On one wall, Wilhelm I confers with Chancellor Bismarck and Field Marshals Moltke and Roon. On the hour, the tower's clock chimes out a melody written by Prince Louis Ferdinand, the Kaiser's great-great-grandson. With their taste for irreverent nicknames,

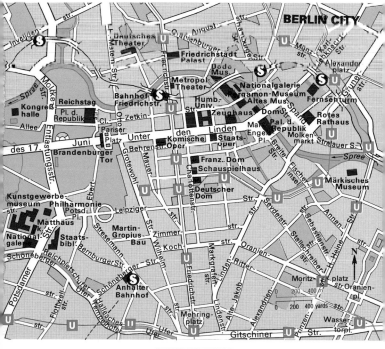

Berliners have deflated the monuments' various imperial or pacifist intentions by dubbing the original church the "broken tooth" and the two main additions the "lipstick" and "powder compact".

Beyond the church is the 22-storey **Europa-Center** between Tauentzienstrasse and Budapester Strasse. There are scores of boutiques, a cinema featuring an excellent 60-minute "multivision" show on Berlin (with an English version), a casino, the famous political cabaret *Die Stachelschweine* ("Porcupines"), discotheques, pubs and a rooftop café with a splendid view across the city. The **Berlin Tourist Office** is on the building's Budapester Strasse side.

More than just a department store, **KaDeWe** on Tauentzienstrasse has achieved the status of a monument. Founded in 1906, long before the Wall, it was not conceived as some Cold War provocation ostentatiously proclaiming western prosperity—even though its full name, Kaufhaus des Westens (Department Store of the West) might suggest otherwise. But that is what its sheer abundance made it look like after 1945. In the weeks following the opening of the Wall, it was a major target for East Germans making their first assault on western consumerism. The food department is phenomenal. At its counters, gourmet globetrotters can perch on a bar stool and sample not only regional food from all over Germany but also Chinese, Japanese, Italian, Russian, French and Swiss meals, served, if you please, with properly chilled champagne.

As zoos go—and many would like to see them go—the **Zoo**, entrance on Budapester Strasse, has one of the most varied collections of animals in Europe. Beyond the colourful pagoda-arched **Elefantentor** (Elephant Gate) are 35 hectares (86 acres) of parkland where you can compare Indian and African elephants, giant pandas from China and rare, single-horned rhinoceroses from India.

TIERGARTEN AREA

Despite its name, the **Tiergarten** (literally "animal garden") is not another zoo. For the Hohenzollern princes, it was a forest for hunting deer and wild boar. After Frederick the Great cleared away the woods to create a formal French garden for his brother August

Ferdinand, it was replanted with trees in the 19th century and transformed into a more natural English-style landscaped park. In World War II, Berliners stripped away the trees again—for fuel. Everything you see today has been planted since 1950, among pleasant boating-ponds, cafés and various monuments.

The **Englischer Garten** beside Altonaer Strasse, financed by British donations, was laid out by the Shropshire Horticultural Society. It forms part of the grounds of **Schloss Bellevue**, a neoclassical palace reconstructed as a residence for the German President.

On the north-west side of the Tiergarten is the **Hansaviertel**, a chic residential neighbourhood rebuilt in 1957 by architects participating in an international design competition, Interbau. Notable among the winners, whose names are inscribed on plaques on each building, are Bauhaus founder Walter Gropius (Händelallee 1–9), Alvar Aalto from Finland (Klopstockstrasse 30) and the Brazilian Oscar Niemeyer (Altonaer Strasse 4–14). The **Akademie der Künste** (Arts Academy), Hanseatenweg 10, holds concerts, plays and exhibitions of avant-garde art. In

front of the building is a bronze *Reclining Figure* by Henry Moore (1956).

On the south side of the Strasse des 17. Juni, overlooking the Landwehr canal, is Ludwig Leo's merry piece of architectural whimsy in bright blue, pink and green. Through its giant tubular elbows, water circulates for the Technical University's deadly earnest **Institut für Wasserbau und Schiffbau** (Hydraulic and Ship Engineering Institute).

At the centre of the park, on the circle of the Grosser Stern, the soaring **Siegessäule** (victory column) is an unabashed monument to Prussian militarism. It was completed in 1873, two years after victory over the French, but also to celebrate successes against Denmark in 1864 and Austria in 1866. Those were the days. The bronze reliefs depicting the victories were fashioned from melted-down cannon and other spoils of war. In 1945, the French insisted they be removed, but let them be restored in 1987 for the city's 750th anniversary celebrations—Germans were beginning to complain about equally bellicose reliefs of Napoleon's victories over the Germans on the Arc de Triomphe in Paris. In a hall at the column's base, mosaics depict the more pacific events leading to Germany's 19th-century unification. A climb of 285 steps takes you to the top of the column for a magnificent city view from beneath the gilded bronze statue of Winged Victory. On the north side of the Grosser Stern are monuments to the architects of that first unification, Chancellor Bismarck and Field Marshals Moltke and Roon.

Directly south of the Siegessäule on the Landwehr canal is the museum of the **Bauhaus-Archiv** (see p. 63), designed by Walter Gropius, founder of Germany's hugely influential Bauhaus school of art, architecture and design. After Weimar and Dessau, the German capital had been the school's last headquarters, under Ludwig Mies van der Rohe, before the Nazis forced its members into exile. Its curving stylized industrial forms make an appropriate start to a tour, east along the canal, of some key monuments of 20th-century architecture.

Note Emil Fahrenkamp's gracefully curved travertine-clad **Bewag building** on the corner of Stauffenbergstrasse, built originally for Shell Oil in 1932 and now the headquarters of the Berlin electric company.

A striking rose and pastel blue sandstone façade dominates the postmodern **Wissenschafts-zentrum** (Science Centre) at Reichpietschufer 48, designed in the 1980s by British architect James Stirling.

At the corner of Potsdamer Strasse, Bauhaus master Mies van der Rohe's design for the **Neue Nationalgalerie** of 19th- and 20th-century art (see p. 62) is a square glass-wall structure with a vast black steel roof supported by eight massive steel columns. This work of characteristic elegant simplicity was completed in 1968, a year before the architect's death. It stands on a raised granite platform that serves as a sculpture court for such huge outdoor pieces as Alexander Calder's *Heads and Tail* and Henry Moore's *Archer* and as a playground for skate-boarders. It can be a little unnerving in the basement galleries to hear the kids thundering over your head, but Mies would not have minded. What counted for him was the purity of a building's form. Function was secondary—the museum's design derives from an idea he originally had for the offices of a Cuban sugar factory.

In dignified isolation beyond the gallery is the slender-steepled neo-Romanesque **St. Matthäus-Kirche**, the only pre-war building hereabouts to survive demolition by Hitler's architect, Albert Speer, or the bombs that followed.

Kulturforum

Between the Potsdamer Bridge and the Tiergarten is the city's Cultural Forum for music and fine arts, incorporating the Neue Nationalgalerie. (The European paintings and sculpture in the Dahlem museums will eventually have a new home here.) Eclipsed by the sober international style imposed by the Bauhaus in the 1920s—of which the Neue Nationalgalerie is a prime example—architect Hans Scharoun was at last able to indulge his taste for Expressionistic free-form structures as mastermind behind the forum's libraries, concert halls and museums (for a detailed description of the museum collections, see p. 62). Scharoun also designed the sprawling **Staatsbibliothek** (State Library), Potsdamerstrasse 33. Despite the library's formidable dimensions, it is a model of peace and harmony. Take advantage of the guided tours available for the public. An ingenious network of staircases leads smoothly to multi-level reading rooms and easily accessible stacks. The library holds photographic and documentary exhibitions and concerts.

Scharoun's intriguing ochre and gold **Philharmonie** (1963), Matthäi-Kirche-Strasse 1, owes its tent-like shape to the demands of the concert hall's acoustics and sight lines. The home of the renowned Berlin Philharmonic Orchestra was designed from the inside out, from the orchestra outwards to the walls and roof. A white-façaded **Kammer-musiksaal** (Chamber Music Hall) has been added to the rear. If you view it from across Tiergartenstrasse, the nearby **Musikinstrumentenmuseum** is reminiscent of an open card-index file.

The **Kunstgewerbemuseum** (Arts and Crafts Museum), Tiergartenstrasse 6, is a rather confusing labyrinth of red brick and white granite but worth a visit for its superb collection of medieval jewellery.

Potsdamer Platz

Reduced by war and the Wall to a bleak no-man's-land, the square that was once as busy as London's Piccadilly Circus or New York's Times Square is coming back to life. Immediately after the destruction of the Wall it became the site of

The four-horse chariot forming the Brandenburg Gate's Quadriga just does not stay put. Napoleon took a liking to it when he rode through the gate in 1806 and shipped it off to Paris. Field Marshal Blücher brought it back again after Waterloo. In 1945 it was melted by Allied fire-bombing and then restored. It was dislodged during the workers' 1953 uprising in East Berlin and resurrected. Its most recent indignity, necessitating yet another restoration, was the vandalism of New Year's Eve revellers after the Wall was opened at the end of 1989. The grand old gate itself makes a natural focus for the city's annual marathon.

ambitious avant-garde art exhibitions or fly-by-night flea markets. Destined now to rival the Ku'damm and Alexanderplatz as a main centre of city life, it is the target of feverish urban planning with projects for prestigious office buildings, commercial centres, art gallery and entertainment complexes.

Nearby, the attractive neo-Renaissance **Martin-Gropius-Bau** at Stresemannstrasse 110 was originally built by Walter Gropius's great-uncle in 1881 as an arts and crafts museum. After an infamous interim as a Gestapo prison under Hitler, it is once again a spacious museum housing in and around its skylighted inner courtyard exhibitions of the Berlinische Galerie, the Werkbund-Archiv and, temporarily, the Jewish Museum (see p. 65).

Down the street at Askanischer Platz is the sad but graceful arcaded ruin of **Anhalter Bahnhof**. By an irony of latterday history, the old railway station was the work of the same architect, Franz Schwechten, that built that other noble ruin, the Kaiser Wilhelm Memorial Church. Today, the wasteland left by the deserted goods yards has become an exotic biotope supporting shrubs and trees foreign to this north-European region, such as the *Robinia* locust tree and St. Lucie cherry. It is also the site of the **Museum für Verkehr und Technik** (Transport and Technology Museum, see p. 65), entrance on Trebbiner Strasse.

The Reichstag

The august parliamentary home of Wilhelminian and Weimar Germany bears the proud dedication *Dem deutschen Volke* (To the German People) on the neoclassical façade built by Paul Wallot in 1894. This appeal to patriotism and democracy set above six Corinthian columns outlasted the burning in 1933 (see p. 22) and the bombs of World War II. Minus the imperial symbolism of the Kaiser's crown on the original glazed dome (both removed by explosives in 1954), the Reichstag reasserted its democratic function on October 3, 1990, when it was the setting for the ceremony of German unity. The interior has been modernized to serve as an assembly for sessions of German parliament. Pending a decision as to whether Berlin is to resume its full role as the permanent seat of national government, the Reichstag also houses a fascinating exhibit: German History under Question *(Fragen an die deutsche Geschichte).* This frank examination of Germany's social and political history from 1800 to the present includes a particularly interesting section on the post-war history of Berlin itself. See how good a command of German John F. Kennedy had in his famous speech in 1963 when he proclaimed, as we see from phonetically written notes, "Ish been ahn Bairleener".

EAST OF BRANDENBURG GATE

Since the momentous changes of November 1989, the centre of what was once the capital of the German Democratic Republic has become an object of curiosity. But the Communist regime's rather pompous governmental buildings and the Stalinist residential architecture of Karl-Marx-Allee take second place to proudly refurbished monuments from the more stylish Prussian era centring on Unter den Linden. Churches and many of the museums are undergoing careful restoration, but the Pergamon, Bode and Märkisches museums are worthy partners to those in the western half of the city.

LAST TRAIN TO SAFETY

The Anhalter Bahnhof's elegant neo-Renaissance façade is a nicely preserved reminder of what was once Berlin's most glamorous railway station, linking the city to Europe's other great capitals. Its west-bound platform staged the tragic last act of the Weimar Republic. Soon after Hitler became Chancellor, Berlin's most gifted artists and intellectuals gathered there—Heinrich Mann, Bertolt Brecht, Kurt Weill, George Grosz, Albert Einstein and other Jewish and left-wing luminaries—their bags packed for exile.

The charm of the old popular boroughs is being only slowly retrieved in Mitte, Prenzlauer Berg, Pankow and Friedrichshain. Meanwhile the Nikolai district is presented as something of a showcase. (Streetnames are likely to change as Communist luminaries are replaced by Prussian predecessors or more recent heroes.)

When you talk with the people, remember that eastern Berlin did not turn into a bastion of anti-Communism overnight. Although the city elected a conservative mayor in December 1990, the successor-party to the

Communists did exceptionally well in the old eastern boroughs, still a solid left-wing stronghold.

Brandenburg Gate

This formidable symbol of the united city seems at last to be realizing the vision of the man who crowned the gate with the Quadriga, a copper statue of Winged Victory in her four-horse chariot. Johann Gottfried Schadow wanted the monument, completed in 1793, to be known as the Gate of Peace *(Friedenstor)* in keeping with the relief of the *Procession of Peace* that he had sculpted beneath the chariot.

The gate itself was designed by Carl Gottfried Langhans. With two rows of six Doric columns forming the gateway proper, it was inspired by the Propylaeum gatehouse leading to the Parthenon in Athens. (To go the whole hog, Hitler had even planned to hoist the gate onto an artificial hill like the Acropolis.) Part of the city wall, the gate was intended by the pragmatic Prussians not as a triumphal arch so much as an imposing tollgate for collecting duties and a control post to stop desertions from the Prussian Army.

Unter den Linden

Sweeping east from the gate, this avenue, literally "Beneath the Linden Trees", was Berlin's grandest. Frederick the Great saw it as the centre of his royal capital, and for the aristocracy and wealthy bourgeoisie it became the most prestigious address in town. Some of its Baroque and neoclassical splendour fell victim to 19th-century building speculation, but the avenue remained fashionable until the bombs of World War II reduced it almost all to rubble. Now the linden trees have been replanted and the most important monumental buildings restored or rebuilt.

Its western end has traditionally been embassy row, dominated on the right, as you come from Brandenburg Gate, by the former Soviet Embassy to the German Democratic Republic. East of Charlottenstrasse, beyond the **Deutsche Staatsbibliothek** (German State Library, 1914), is Frederick the Great's architectural complex known as "Forum Fridericianum" and renamed by the East Germans **Lindenforum**. On the avenue's centre strip is imposing equestrian statue of Frederick the Great (1851) by Christian Daniel Rauch.

To recreate the cultural and intellectual climate that his grandfather had brought to Berlin in the 17th century, the king commissioned a new building to house the Royal Academy, a library, an opera house and a palace for his brother, Prince Heinrich. This admirable classical architectural testament has been beautifully restored. Heinrich's palace (1753) forms part of **Humboldt-Universität**. The institution founded in 1810 counted among its professors and students the Grimm brothers, Hegel, Engels, Marx and Einstein. Opposite its rather severe classicism is the curving Baroque façade of the **Alte Bibliothek** (Old Library), nicknamed by Berliners the *Kommode* (chest of drawers).

Across Bebelplatz is Knobelsdorff's grand Palladian-style **Deutsche Staatsoper** (German State Opera). The **Operncafé** is housed in the Prinzessinnenpalais, the Baroque town-house of the Prussian princesses. Since reunification, its open-air terrace has become one of the most popular rendezvous in eastern Berlin.

The 19th-century statues by Christian Daniel Rauch of German military heroes in battles against Napoleon—Blücher, Gneisenau and Yorck—were resurrected by the East Germans to reaffirm the Prussian military tradition. Beside the university, the old Prussian army guardhouse, the Doric-porticoed **Neue Wache** (New Guardhouse) was Karl Friedrich Schinkel's first important neoclassical design, completed in 1818. Next door is the handsome Baroque **Zeughaus**, once arsenal for the Prussian Army, as the sculpted suits of armour testify along the roof. It now houses part of the reunited city's **Museum für Deutsche Geschichte** (German History Museum). Andreas Schlüter provided the military sculpture, but as a member of the Mennonite sect he was able to assert his pacifist views with his poignant sculpted masks of dying warriors (1696), in the inner courtyard named after him, the Schlüterhof.

South of the Staatsoper is **St. Hedwigs-Kathedrale**, a massive domed structure built in the 18th century for the Catholics incorporated into Protestant Prussia by Frederick's conquest of Polish Silesia.

The celebrated architectural ensemble on the Gendarmenmarkt, at present Platz der Akademie, is being meticulously restored. The imposing **Schiller-Denkmal** (1868), a monument sculpted in Carrara marble, surrounds the writer with the muses of poetry, drama, history and philosophy. It stands in front of Schinkel's noble Ionic-porticoed **Schauspielhaus** (Playhouse), now a concert hall. The edifice provides a harmonious link between the **Französischer Dom** (French Cathedral) to the north, built for Berlin's immigrant Huguenots, and the **Deutscher Dom** (German Cathedral) to the south, both early 18th-century. The twin domes were added in 1785.

Karl-Liebknecht-Strasse

Nineteenth-century statues of warriors and victory goddesses decorate **Marx-Engels Bridge** linking Unter den Linden to Karl-Liebknecht-Strasse. From the bridge, designed by Schinkel as the Schlossbrücke (Palace Bridge), look left to the monumental **Museumsinsel**, the site of eastern Berlin's most prestigious museums, described on pp. 69–73. Beyond the bridge, **Marx-Engels-Platz** was laid out as the equivalent of Red Square, the focus of the Communists' May Day military parades and mass rallies. The Hohenzollern's war-damaged Stadtschloss (City Palace) once stood here, until Walter Ul-bricht decided to raze it as symbolizing German imperialism, despite art historians' protests that it was the city's most significant Baroque building.

The palace where Spartacist leader Karl Liebknecht proclaimed his abortive "Socialist Republic" was replaced by the vast bronze glass, steel and marble **Palast der Republik** (closed in 1990 due to cases of asbestos poisoning). It housed East Germany's parliament and a 5,000-seat conference hall where the Party congresses were held. Conceived as a "house for the people", it also contains restaurants, cafés, discotheque and bowling alley.

The structure's extravagant populism is countered across the street by the pomposity of Kaiser Wilhelm II's monstrous **Berliner Dom**. Prussian Berlin was full of cathedrals. This one has a crypt for 95 Hohenzollern sarcophagi.

Continue along Karl-Liebknecht-Strasse to the 13th-century **Marienkirche** on Neuer Markt, a haven of sober Gothic simplicity amidst the prevailing

French Huguenot refugees found a safe haven here. This, the Französischer Dom, was their cathedral.

THE ABSENT MONUMENT

It's gone, but not forgotten. No monument could more forcefully capture the public imagination by its sheer ugliness, no structure more explicitly convey its historical meaning than the Berlin Wall. Fragments of *die Mauer* "decorate" mantlepieces and museums all over the world, but the city in which it was erected has done everything possible to obliterate if not its memory then at least its physical trace. No one who witnessed its construction and poisonous effect on daily life needs a souvenir.

This barrier against free passage from East to West traced West Berlin's 162-km. (100-mile) border with East Berlin and the East German hinterland. Masterminded by Erich Honecker when he was still No. 2 to Walter Ulbricht, the Wall grew from an improvised barbed-wire fence into a massive barrier 4 m. (13 ft.) high, topped by concrete tubing to prevent easy hand-holds. Behind it, protected by an electrified fence, stretched a strip of sand 150 m. (160 yd.) wide—a no-man's-land equipped with watch towers, tank traps, patrol dogs, searchlights and a ditch 5 m. (16 ft.) deep to stop vehicles breaking through.

Civilian escapes by tunnel, cars with hidden compartments and other subterfuges planned by professional mercenaries or desperate amateurs became as much a part of Cold War legend as break-outs by military prisoners were in World War II.

The western side of the Wall was embellished with graffiti emphasizing its grotesqueness with humour or pathos—*Lieber Rotwein als Totsein* (Better red wine than lyin' dead), *Menschen, ich habe Euch lieb* (People, I love you)—or the anger of unprintable curses against East Germany.

The most poignant stretch of the barrier was in the northern district of Wedding where Bernauerstrasse ran directly along the border, one side of the street in West and the other in East Berlin. In the first days after the border was closed in August 1961, people jumped from first- or second-storey windows until workmen bricked them up and later dynamited the houses down to ground-floor façades incorporated into the Wall.

And yet the East German Communists tried for years to persuade the world this was an "anti-Fascist protective rampart" *(Antifaschistischer Schutzwall)*, then, more respectably, a "modern frontier" *(moderne Grenze)*. It ended up as a gigantic quarry for squalid ornaments.

bombast. Inside, see Andreas Schlüter's Baroque marble pulpit (1703) and a late-Gothic fresco of the *Dance of Death* (1484) in the tower hall.

The neo-Renaissance **Rotes Rathaus** (Red Town Hall) owes its name to its red clinker masonry, not its ideology. Built in 1869, it expresses with a certain style the town's pride when Prussia was top-of-the-world, a pride revived now that it is once more the seat of the united municipal government.

Beyond the huge **Neptunbrunnen** (Fountain of Neptune)—not that you could miss it—is the **Fernsehturm** (Television Tower), with an Information Centre on the ground floor. Built in 1969, at 365 m. (1,197 ft.) it tops the Eiffel Tower by 65 m. (213 ft.) and absolutely dwarfs western Berlin's Funkturm, which was the object of the exercise. It looks like a billiard cue that has miraculously skewered one of the balls. The observation deck and café are in the ball, 207 m. (679 ft.) up. The view is great and the café revolves.

Nikolaiviertel

Around Molkenmarkt south of the Rotes Rathaus, the Nikolai neighbourhood was restored for the city's 750th anniversary

celebrations in 1987 as a rather "clean" example of Old Berlin. Site of Berlin's earliest settlement (see p. 13), it clusters around the city's oldest parish church, the twin-steepled Gothic **Nikolaikirche**. The church was built in 1230 and now serves as part of the **Märkisches Museum** (see p. 73), devoted to the city's history. Among the buildings typical of Berlin's 1900s resurrected here is the **Gaststätte Zum Nussbaum**, the favourite tavern of famed cartoonist Heinrich Zille. More stately is the reconstructed **Ephraimpalais**, Poststrasse 16, a Rococo mansion built for Friedrich II's Jewish financier Veitel Heine Ephraim in 1767. Besides providing a delightful setting for chamber-music recitals, it is used for exhibitions of 18th and 19th-century art and Berlin history.

Alexanderplatz

"Alex", as the huge square is known, was once the undisputed heart of Berlin and somehow retains the magic spirit of the city despite relentless post-war modernization. Now a bustling pedestrian area of cafés, hotels, department stores and apartment blocks, Alex has always been the hub of night-and-day life, celebrated in

Alfred Döblin's great 1929 novel *Berlin Alexanderplatz*. On the south side of the square, two buildings survive from that era, the **Berolinahaus** municipal offices and **Alexanderhaus** department store. They were designed by Peter Behrens, dynamic master builder whose pupils included Le Corbusier, Gropius and Mies van der Rohe.

His lessons were disregarded by the designers of the bleak apartments, hotels and shops along **Karl-Marx-Allee** leading south-east from Alex. Drive up and down it if only for the reminder of what soulless buildings Stalinist architecture could produce. Until 1961 the street was named Stalinallee.

North of Alexanderplatz, behind the popular Volksbühne theatre, **Schönhauser Allee** is one of the most characteristic avenues of old Berlin leading to the centre of the working-class quarter of **Prenzlauer Berg**. Four- and five-storey tenements are interspersed with decaying mansions in the heartland of eastern Berlin's *Alternativen* community, where you will also

Once a royal hideaway in Charlottenburg Palace gardens, the Belvedere now encases a collection of porcelain.

find some of the town's most interesting bars. On **Husemann-strasse,** a number of shops from the age of Kaiser Wilhelm II have been nicely restored.

On Schönhauser Allee you'll find the **Jewish Cemetery** (*Judischen Friedhof*), the resting place of German Impressionist painter Max Lieber-mann and the opera composer Giacomo Meyerbeer. The neo-Byzantine **Synagogue** at Ryke-strasse 53 was one of the rare Jewish buildings to survive the 1938 Kristallnacht pogrom, as it was tucked away at the back of an inner courtyard.

In the borough of Pankow at the north end of Schönhauser Allee, **Schloss Niederschön-hausen** is a handsome Baroque palace with English landscaped gardens, destined to be opened to the public after many years of being off-limits as an official government residence.

SCHLOSS CHARLOTTENBURG

The carefully restored palace, an exemplary piece of Prussian Baroque and Rococo architecture and decoration, is the city's only surviving major Hohen-zollern residence. (See p. 66 for a description of the palace's

Gallery of Romantic Art and the Egyptian and Classical Antiquity museums in the same neighbourhood.)

Schloss Charlottenburg was conceived as a summer retreat for the future Queen Sophie Charlotte in the 1690s, when the site beside the Spree river west of the Tiergarten lay well outside the city limits. It was a little palace—scarcely one-fifth of the huge structure you see today. Only with the addition of a majestic domed tower with the goddess Fortune as its weathervane, the Orangerie to the west and a new east wing did it become big enough for Frederick the Great. If he had to leave his beloved Potsdam, this was where he came.

In the palace courtyard is a powerful **equestrian statue** (1697) of the Great Elector Friedrich Wilhelm, designed by Andreas Schlüter. One of many art works lost in World War II, it was recovered in 1949 from Tegel harbour, where it had sunk with the barge that was taking it to safety. It originally stood beside the ill-fated Stadtschloss (see p. 46), also designed by Schlüter.

To recapture the interior's gracious Rococo atmosphere, furnishings and decoration from other 18th-century Prussian palaces have replaced what was irretrievably destroyed here during the war. You are free to roam at will through the Hohenzollerns' ornate world, except for Friedrich I's and Sophie Charlotte's apartments in the central building and west wing, for which there are regular guided tours.

In the **Gobelinzimmer**, notice the fine 18th-century tapestries by Charles Vigne, and in the **Rotes Tressenzimmer** two exquisite blue and white Meissen vases. The rays of light on the ceiling of the **Audienzzimmer** (Reception Room) and dazzling yellow damask walls in the **Schlafzimmer** (bedroom) imitate the obsessive motif of Louis XIV, the Sun King, the Prussian rulers' hero. Chinoiserie dominates the opulent **Porzellankabinett**, filled with hundreds of pieces of Chinese and Japanese porcelain, including life-size figures of mandarins. The relatively sober **Japanische Kammer** has some prized lacquered cabinets and tables. The tapestries depict, despite the chamber's name, landscapes of China. Chamber music recitals are held in the **Eichengalerie** (Oak Gallery) and the **Eosander-Kapelle** (chapel) with an extravagant Rococo decor that makes it more theatre than place of worship.

The east wing designed for Frederick the Great by his favourite architect, Georg von Knobelsdorff, subtly combines dignified late-Baroque façades with exuberant Rococo interiors. Part of the ground floor is at present given over to the **Galerie der Romantik** (Gallery of Romantic Art)—due to be moved to the Museumsinsel or the Kulturforum. The ceremonial staircase leading to Frederick the Great's state apartments has an abstract modern ceiling fresco by Hann Trier in place of the original Rococo decor destroyed by fire. Trier also painted the ceiling of the **Weisse Saal** (throne room and banquet hall).

The finest achievement of Knobelsdorff at Charlottenburg is the spacious **Goldene Galerie** in gilt and green marble. It leads to the two rooms boasting a remarkable group of eight **Watteau paintings.** Frederick the Great was amused by the Frenchman's somewhat insolent *Enseigne du Gersaint*, a shop sign for art dealer Gersaint, in which a portrait of Louis XIV is being unceremoniously packed away. Other superb works include *L'amour paisible* (Quiet Love), *Les Bergers* (The Shepherds) and *L'Embarquement pour Cythère* (Embarkation for Cythera).

The palace's formal French gardens juxtapose English landscaping. Among the many buildings in the grounds, nearest to the palace is the pretty little 19th-century neoclassical **Schinkel-Pavillon.** See upstairs an amusing panorama of 1830s Berlin by Eduard Gaertner. North of the carp pond, the Baroque **Belvedere**, originally a tea house, is now a Berlin Porcelain Museum. A Doric temple provides a **Mausoleum** for Hohenzollerns of the 19th century.

OLYMPIASTADION AND I.C.C.

Two monstrous buildings command our attention west of Charlottenburg. Hitler's **Olympiastadion**, built for the Games of 1936, was spared bombardment to serve as headquarters for the British Army. The structure's bombastic gigantism is eloquent testimony to the Führer's architectural taste. From the main Olympic Gate, it looks remarkably "low slung" until you see inside that the field itself has been sunk 12 m. (40 ft.) below ground level.

Still used for sporting events and open daily to the public, the stadium was originally built for 120,000 spectators—the whole complex being conceived for half a million.

On Masurenallee south-east of the stadium, another colossus, the **I.C.C.** *(Internationales Congress Centrum),* presents German technological know-how and commercial power wrapped in an aluminium skin. The complex has 80 conference halls and meeting rooms for 400 congresses each year. A guided tour reveals the building's ingenuity and formidable efficiency. Hall 1, the biggest, seats 5,000, but Hall 2 is the most fun. At the press of a button, a convention hall with tiered seating rises and disappears into the ceiling to reveal within minutes a banquet room for 4,000 diners. Conference delegates are each equipped with individual microphones—press a button and a mike pops up from the arm of your seat—as well as built-in facilities for simultaneous translation in any of eight languages. It comes almost as a disappointment that there are no seat belts and the thing does not fly.

Amidst all this gigantism, the **Funkturm** (Radio Tower) on the neighbouring exhibition grounds *(Messegelände)* seems positively tiny—150 m. (492 ft.) to the tip of its antenna, half the size of the TV Tower in eastern Berlin. But for the view, take the lift to the restaurant, 55 m. (180 ft.) up, or the observation platform at the top. Look south-west down the stretch of Autobahn known acronymically as the **Avus** (from *Automobil-, Verkehrs- und Übungsstrasse*—Automobile, Traffic and Training Road). Built in 1921, it was Germany's first racetrack, a simple 8-km. (5-mi.) two-way straight with a loop at either end. Record speed was Rudolf Caracciola's 396 kph (246 mph) in a Mercedes. No longer for racing, it now links the city centre to the westbound Autobahn.

GRUNEWALD AND WANNSEE

The pre-war dense pine forest, largely stripped for fuel in 1945, has been replanted, adding to the 18 million pines some 6 million chestnut, linden, beech, birch and oak trees. The wooded areas form a reserve for deer, wild boar, marten, foxes and myriad rabbits, but there are plenty of green meadows for picnics.

Buses and trains serve the forest and lakes. Drivers take the Avus and turn off on the Hüttenweg to **Grunewaldsee**, a lake offering good swimming off sandy beaches. On the east shore, in a pretty lakeside setting of beech trees, the **Jagdschloss Grunewald** was a hunting lodge built in 1542 for Prince Elector Joachim II and later baroquified. A good collection of German and Dutch paintings includes works by Jordaens, Rubens, Bruyn and Lucas Cranach. The portrait of Prince Joachim is by Cranach's son.

On the Grunewald's west side, via Havelchaussee, ferry stations offer boat rides on the Havel river and forest lakes. The east bank of the Havel is lined with pleasant sandy beaches all the way down to the Wannsee lakes (the region's subsoil is natural sand). **Strandbad Wannsee** is Berlin's biggest beach. With its promenades, restaurants and hooded wicker beach shelters, Wannsee is comparable in atmosphere to smart resorts on Germany's North Sea coast.

West of the Grosser Wannsee, Königsstrasse crosses Berliner Forst, an extension of the Grunewald to **Kleinglienicke Park**. Its whimsical landscaping of little hills and dells, bridges and ponds was the work of Peter Josef Lenné in the early 19th century. The **palace** (1828) is a rather austere neo-classical edifice by Schinkel but the nearby cloister, villa and garden houses add a romantic touch.

TEUFELSBERG, DEVIL'S MOUNTAIN

At the beginning of the Grunewald, in the middle of the flat northern European plain that stretches from Warsaw to the Netherlands, is a mountain. Aptly named Teufelsberg (Devil's Mountain), it is small, only 115 m. (380 ft.) high—but a mountain nonetheless, created by a pile of rubble from World War II bombardments.

In summer, the hill is nicely grassed over for toddler mountain climbers to scramble on or hang-gliders to jump from. In winter, snow creates an excellent toboggan run, a good nursery slope for skiers and even two bone-rattling ski jumps. Just how flat that north European plain is east of this mountain is demonstrated by the off-limits summit where military radar equipment is said to operate all the way to Asia.

A ferry links **Pfaueninsel** (Peacock Island), a delightfully tranquil nature reserve in the Havel, to the northern edge of Berliner Forst. Venerable oaks and giant Californian lodgepole pines remain from an arboretum created in the 18th century. The island menagerie served to stock Berlin Zoo, but the **bird sanctuary** still has much to offer the nature lover, including, of course, peacocks. At the south tip, half hidden in the trees, is Schinkel's Swiss Cottage, but the island's principal curiosity is the fake ruin **Schloss Pfaueninsel**. It was built in 1797 as a hideaway for Friedrich Wilhelm II and his mistress, Countess Wilhelmine von Lichtenau. The white wooden façade imitates granite blocks, and the sweet little turrets (one capped by a bright blue dome) are linked at the top by a pretty, but rather flimsy-looking bridge. The façade's arched gateway seems to lead to an idyllic landscape, but it is just a painted niche, more make-believe. Take a look inside the palace at Anton Graff's portrait of

From her window in Spandau, the lady remembers a Berlin quite different from that of its bright and brittle youth.

COMING IN FROM THE COLD

Spy exchanges are, of course, usually done in secret. But one cold dawn in 1962, the international press had been alerted: the American U-2 pilot Gary Powers was being traded for ace Soviet spy Colonel Rudolf Abel. Big black cars rolled up on opposite sides of the Glienicker Bridge. The Americans took Abel to the middle of the bridge, where the Russians examined him to make sure the merchandise was genuine and in good condition. At the same time, the Americans were busy checking Powers. Everything was O.K. and the deal was completed. Meanwhile, under the bridge, the swans swam back and forth from east to west, with nobody checking.

Friedrich Wilhelm—hard to imagine this gloomy fellow being so playful.

Königsstrasse extends to an illustrious relic of the Cold War, Glienicker Bridge, once a highly restricted border crossing between West Berlin and East Germany where the KGB and CIA exchanged their spies. It is now a convenient road link between Berlin and Potsdam.

SPANDAU AND REINICKENDORF

The north-western boroughs of Spandau and Reinickendorf constitute a rural world far removed from the city centre's bustle. This quiet area of meadows, farms and villages-within-the-city provides Berliners with an escape from urban stress.

With a history longer than Berlin's, **Spandau** still remains fiercely independent-minded. It was the most reluctant of the townships to be annexed by the metropolis in 1920, and residents still ask taxi drivers to take them "to Berlin" when going to the city centre.

The **Altstadt** (old town) at the confluence of the Havel and Spree rivers was less hurt by bombardment than the rest of Berlin and retains much of its former charm. You will see a few gabled houses, Renaissance façades, even traces of the 14th-century town wall along Hoher Weg, east of Falkenseer Platz. Spandauers claim that **St. Nikolai-Kirche** on Reformationsplatz is where Prince Joachim II converted to the Protestant faith. The much-restored brick Gothic structure has an imposing Renaissance altar.

The 16th-century **Zitadelle** in the Havel river was the scene of heavy fighting during the Napoleonic Wars. Its walls enclose the old **Juliusturm**, a castle keep from prior medieval fortifications. It was the repository for gold coins paid by the French as reparations after the Franco-Prussian War and returned as part payment for reparations after World War I.

Following the death of its last inmate, Rudolf Hess, in 1987, the Spandau prison for Nazi war criminals was razed to make way for a community centre.

To the north of the borough, **Spandau Forst** is half the size of the Grunewald, but just as lovely. The forest incorporates nature reserves where rare plants are protected in their wild state; **Teufelsbruch**, which regularly records Berlin's coldest winter temperatures, provides a natural shelter for shrubs and flowers from the sub-Arctic tundra. Just east of Teufelsbruch, summer bathing and camping are popular at **Bürgerablage** beach on the Havel river.

Reinickendorf takes in Tegel airport and **Märkisches Viertel**, one of the city's most controversial residential developments. Housing 50,000 people who previously lived in aging tenements, it served at first as an object lesson in how not to realize a modern urban project. It was launched in the 60s with the slogan: "We want to create flowers and fairy tales—more Beatles, less Greeks," but the skyscraper blocks of flats were deemed too high and too impersonal, provision for open spaces and public transport inadequate. Now a new park has been laid out, using more of that World War II rubble. The bus service has been improved and a new U-Bahn line promised.

Tegeler See, Reinickendorf's lake, has good facilities for swimming, boating and hiking. Boats leave from the Greenwich-Promenade pier for cruises down the Havel to Potsdam via Glienicker Bridge.

For a real taste of rustic life without leaving Berlin, visit the farming community of **Lübars.** This veritable medieval village has preserved its peasant cottages. The charming single storey dwellings with white stucco façades nestle against a grass-covered mound on which rises the village church. This sober Baroque structure with a graceful steeple was rebuilt in 1793 after a village fire. And around the village stretch the wheat and barley fields where these metropolitan farmers make a living.

EVERYTHING HAS ITS PRICE

Spandau suffered no more damage in World War II than it did at the hands of Napoleon's soldiers retreating from Russia in 1813. Prussian and Russian forces together laid siege to 3,000 French troops occupying Spandau Citadel. Berliners rode out to watch the fighting, keeping outside the range of the cannonade that was setting fire to scores of Spandau houses.

After the rout of the French, Berliners wanted to visit the citadel and take a peek at the burned-out houses. The people of Spandau charged admission and collected 4,335 thalers, which they used to rebuild their homes.

KÖPENICK

The borough of Köpenick, with its delightful **Altstadt** (old town) of 18th- and 19th-century houses, lies on the southern outskirts of eastern Berlin. Like Spandau in the west, Köpenick has a longer history than Berlin itself, having been a

Slav settlement on an island in the Spree from the 9th century. It has a similarly independent-minded history. Socialist before the proclamation of the Weimar Republic, the town led the counter-assault which ended the right-wing Kapp Putsch of 1920 (see p. 19). Local workers' resistance to Hitler in May 1933 led to the *Köpenicker Blutwoche* (blood-bath) in which storm troopers killed 91 workers.

The sturdy 17th-century **Schloss Köpenick** occupies its own little island in the Dahme river. It houses a **Kunstge-werbemuseum** (Arts and Crafts Museum) noted for an excellent collection of medieval gold jewellery, Meissen porcelain, Venetian glass and 18th-century Rococo furniture.

From Köpenick, a branch of the Spree leads to the **Grosser Müggelsee**, Berlin's largest lake, very pleasant for boat cruises or picnics on the shore. On the east side of the lake is the charming old fishing village of **Rahnsdorf** where single-storey stucco-façaded cottages line the tranquil Dorfstrasse.

The rustic "village" of Lübars is a world apart—within the city limits.

MUSEUMS

Like everything else in Germany, Berlin's museum scene is in a state of flux. With expansion of the Kulturforum (see p. 39) and changes brought about by German unification, Berlin is reorganizing its art collections. After 1945, many works originally in the eastern half of the city or Potsdam found a new home in the west. As the museums of eastern Berlin are renovated, some paintings and sculptures may move again, in both directions. Our descriptions keep the best possible account of the flux. We have grouped them according to their main locations: in western Berlin, the Tiergarten, Kreuzberg, Dahlem and Charlottenburg; in eastern Berlin, the Museumsinsel, plus the Märkisches Museum on the south side of the Spree with its associated museums in the Nikolaiviertel.

Tiergarten

Neue Nationalgalerie

(Potsdamer Strasse 50, closed Monday.) The ground floor is used for temporary exhibitions, with the permanent collections of 19th- and 20th-century art on the lower level. After the catastrophic Nazi confiscation of "Degenerate Art", the gallery is gradually rebuilding its modern collection. (The Galerie der Romantik, at present in Schloss Charlottenberg, is to be incorporated in an annexe.)

German painting: Adolph Menzel depicts the rise of 19th-century Germany with his *Berlin-Potsdam Railway* (1847) and Wilhelm I's *Departure for the Army* (1871). Lovis Corinth has a tenderly observed *Donna Gravida* (1909), Max Slevogt a striking *Still Life with Lemons* (1921) and Max Liebermann a penetrating *Self-Portrait* (1925). Outstanding among the Expressionists: Edvard Munch's *Life Frieze* (1906), Max Beckmann's *Woman's Bath* (1919), the Otto Dix portrait of *Art Dealer Alfred Flechtheim* (1926) and George Grosz's *Pillars of Society* (1926).

French painting: three landscapes by Courbet, notably *Falaises d'Etretat* (1870); Monet's *St.-Germain-l'Auxerrois* (1866), Manet's *Au Jardin d'Hiver* (1879), van Gogh's *Moulin de la Galette* (1886) and works by Renoir and Bonnard.

American painting: important works by Jackson Pollock, Mark Rothko, Barnett Newman and Frank Stella.

Bauhaus-Archiv

(Klingelhöferstrasse 13, closed Tuesday.) The museum documents the achievements of Europe's most progressive 20th-century school of architecture and design. It was established in Weimar in 1919, transferred to Dessau and briefly to Berlin before Hitler drove it into exile in 1933, where it regrouped in Chicago and Cambridge, Massachusetts. Architects Walter Gropius, Mies van der Rohe and Marcel Breuer and artists Paul Klee, Vasili Kandinsky, Oskar Schlemmer, Lyonel Feininger and Laszlo Moholy-Nagy sought to integrate the arts, crafts and architecture into the 20th century's mass industrial society.

On view is a selection of objects they created: tubular steel chairs, desks, teapots, cups and saucers, new weaves for carpets, chess pieces and children's building blocks. And of course pioneering designs for factories, schools, housing projects, even newspaper kiosks. One of the most beautiful architectural models is Mies van der Rohe's 30-storey glass skyscraper in the shape of a cloverleaf. The 1921 project was never realized, but proved its enduring modernity when a variation was built in 1968 in Chicago by Mies's pupils.

Kunstgewerbemuseum

(Tiergartenstrasse 6, closed Monday.) Outstanding in the Arts and Crafts Museum's dazzling collection of jewellery is the **Welfenschatz** (Guelphs' treasure). These examples of the goldsmith's art from the 11th to 15th centuries—richly bejewelled crosses, reliquaries and portable altars—were presented to St. Blasius Cathedral in Brunswick by succeeding generations of Guelph dukes. Other prized exhibits include

TEDDY BEARS' PICNIC

If you go down to the Ku'damm today, you don't have to go in disguise. For every bear that ever there was is gathered there for certain because Ku'damm Karree shopping centre (Kurfürstendamm 206) has a terrific Teddy Bear Museum. See the earliest Teddy (1900) on iron wheels, pulled by a chain. Thereafter, the bears are liberated—Paddington, Winnie the Pooh and Rupert are all there, along with Germany's wide-eyed Steiff, Rolls-Royce of stuffed bears.

glazed Italian majolica and a bewitching array of porcelain—Chinese, Meissen, Frankenthaler, Nymphenburger and Berlin's own Königliche Porzellan Manufaktur (the royal KPM).

Musikinstrumenten-Museum

(Tiergartenstrasse 1, closed Monday.) Among the museum's many historical musical instruments are a 1703 Stradivarius violin and the 1810 piano of composer Carl Maria von Weber, as well as a monumental Wurlitzer cinema organ from New York, 1929.

Kreuzberg

Berlin Museum

(Lindenstrasse 14, closed Monday.) The museum of municipal history, folklore and culture is housed in a nicely restored Baroque building, remarkably cheerful for what was once the Kammergericht (Supreme Court). Models of the old city show how Berlin has grown over eight centuries. Authentically furnished rooms illustrate the life of the Berlin bourgeoisie from the assertive age of neoclassical architect Karl Friedrich Schinkel (late 18th century to 1840), the solid Biedermeier days of the mid-19th century, the ponderous Gründerzeit (founding era of Germany's first unification), the lighter period of Jugendstil and the years leading up to World War I. The clothes fashions of the times are especially well treated and there is a charming collection of toys.

Berlinische Galerie

(Stresemannstrasse 110, closed Monday.) The gallery is located in the Martin-Gropius-Bau, a handsome 1881 building designed by a great-uncle of Bauhaus master Walter Gropius. It illustrates Berlin life from 1870 to the present day through the eyes of the city's leading artists. Beginning solemnly with Hohenzollern court painter Anton von Werner, the collection presents a razor-sharp view of the city from Impressionists Max Liebermann and Lovis Corinth, Expressionists Otto Dix and Conrad Felixmüller, the vitriolic social critics of the 1920s, George Grosz and John Heartfield, to the abstracts and photorealists of the contemporary era, including foreign Berlin residents like American Ed Kienholz or Hungarian Laszlo Lakner.

RECOMMENDED HOTELS

We give below a selection of hotels in three price categories, grouped in four areas: Berlin City, west; Charlottenburg; Kreuzberg; and Berlin City, east. To be on the safe side, book in advance, either through your travel agent or directly with the hotel. We have included phone numbers and, wherever possible, fax numbers too.

As a basic guide to room prices, we have used the following symbols (for a double room with bath, including breakfast):

▮ below DM 180   ▮▮ DM 180–240   ▮▮▮ above DM 240

BERLIN CITY, WEST

Artemisia Frauenhotel ▮▮
Brandenburgische Str. 18, 1000 Berlin 15. Tel. 87 89 05, fax 214 28 26
Small, quiet hotel garni for women, with facilities for children.

Askanischer Hof ▮▮
Kurfürstendamm 53, 1000 Berlin 15. Tel. 881 80 33, tlx 181550
Small, family-run hotel garni in quiet location. Delightful 1900s atmosphere; very friendly reception. Children welcome.

Berlin Mark Hotel ▮▮
Meinekestr. 18, 1000 Berlin 15. Tel. 88 00 20, fax 88 00 28 04
217 rooms. Well-situated family hotel with young atmosphere. Bistro with terrace.

Bristol-Hotel Kempinski ▮▮▮
Kurfürstendamm 27, 1000 Berlin 15. Tel. 88 43 40, fax 883 60 75
Large, luxurious international hotel with excellent facilities: conference rooms, solarium, sauna, several restaurants, baby-sitting, indoor swimming pool. Comfortable, sound-proofed rooms.

Grand Hotel Esplanade ▋▋▋▋

Lützowufer 15, 1000 Berlin 30. Tel. 26 10 11, fax 262 91 21
400 rooms. No charge for children up to 12 sharing parents' room. Resident doctor; library with 4,000 art books.

Hotel Astoria ▋▋

Fasanenstr. 2, 1000 Berlin 12. Tel. 312 40 67, fax 312 50 27
33 rooms. Hotel garni. Special rates for children under 12. Baby-sitting facilities, airport bus, hotel yacht.

Hotel Domus ▋

Uhlandstr. 49, 1000 Berlin 15. Tel. 88 20 41, fax 882 04 10
93 rooms. Quiet, central hotel garni.

Hotel Eden ▋

Sächsische Str. 70, 1000 Berlin 15. Tel. 882 20 66, fax 882 57 61
63 rooms. Quiet hotel garni with traditional atmosphere. No charge for children under 12 sharing parents' room.

Hotel Heidelberg ▋

Knesebeckstr. 15, 1000 Berlin 12. Tel. 31 01 03, fax 313 58 70
40 rooms. Family-run hotel garni; quietly situated near Savigny-Platz. Facilities for children. Airport bus.

Hotel Inter-Continental ▋▋▋▋

Budapester Str. 2, 1000 Berlin 30. Tel. 2 60 20, fax 260 28 07 60
600 rooms. Two restaurants. Indoor swimming pool, sauna. Facilities for business travellers. View over Tiergarten.

Hotel Lichtburg ▋▋

Paderborner Str. 10, 1000 Berlin 15. Tel. 891 80 41, tlx 184208
66 rooms. Quiet. Baby-sitting and special diets upon request.

Hotel Meineke ▋

Meinekestr. 10, 1000 Berlin 15. Tel. 88 28 11, fax 882 57 16
66 rooms. Quiet, friendly hotel garni with large, comfortable rooms.

Hotel Palace ▋▋▋▋

Budapester Str. 42, 1000 Berlin 30. Tel. 25 49 70, fax 262 65 77
258 rooms. Spacious, well-fitted rooms. Children welcome.

Hotel-Pension Juwel   ▮
Meinekestr. 26, 1000 Berlin 15. Tel. 882 71 41
18 rooms. Family-run hotel garni. Baby-sitter. Quiet, historic location.

Steigenberger Hotel   ▮▮▮
Los-Angeles-Platz 1, 1000 Berlin 30. Tel. 2 10 80, fax 210 81 17
400 rooms. Conference facilities. Sauna, solarium. Central.

CHARLOTTENBURG

Hotel am Studio   ▮
Kaiserdamm 80, 1000 Berlin 19. Tel. 30 20 81, fax 301 95 78
77 rooms. Hotel garni. Special rates for children.

Hotel Ibis   ▮
Messedamm 10, 1000 Berlin 19. Tel. 30 39 30, fax 301 95 36
191 rooms. Hotel garni. Special rates for children. Conference facilities.

Hotel Heinz Kardell   ▮
Gervinusstr. 24, 1000 Berlin 12. Tel. 324 10 66
33 rooms. Near Charlottenburg S-Bahn station. Quiet, family-run.
International restaurant; special diets on request.

Hotel Seehof   ▮▮▮
Lietzensee-Ufer 11, 1000 Berlin 19. Tel. 32 00 20, fax 32 00 22 51
77 rooms. Attractive hotel on lake shore. Conference facilities.

Kanthotel   ▮
Kantstr. 111, 1000 Berlin 12. Tel. 32 30 26, fax 324 09 52
55 rooms. Family-run hotel garni. Baby-sitting, rooms for handicapped
guests, conference facilities. Special rates for children and weekends.

Pension Seeblick   ▮
Neue Kantstr. 14, 1000 Berlin 19. Tel. 321 30 72
9 rooms. Family-run pension overlooking lake. Excellent breakfast.

Schlossparkhotel   ▮▮
Heubnerweg 2a, 1000 Berlin 19. Tel. 322 40 61, fax 891 99 42
39 rooms. Quiet location near Charlottenburg palace gardens, swimming
pool, conference facilities.

KREUZBERG

Hervis Hotel International ▮▮
Stresemannstr. 97–103, 1000 Berlin 61. Tel. 261 14 44, fax 261 50 27
73 rooms. Quiet, modern hotel garni near Anhalter Bahnhof. Conference facilities. No charge for children under 12 sharing parents' room.

Hotel Transit ▮
Hagelberger Str. 53, 1000 Berlin 61. Tel. 785 50 51
Inexpensive hotel with young atmosphere. Dormitory accommodation available.

Riehmers Hofgarten ▮
Yorckstr. 83, 1000 Berlin 61. Tel. 78 10 11, fax 786 60 59
26 rooms. Hotel garni.

BERLIN CITY, EAST

Domhotel ▮▮▮
Mohrenstr. 30, 1080 Berlin. Tel. 2 09 80, fax 20 98 82 69
370 rooms. Modern hotel on historic site near Platz der Akademie.

Grand Hotel ▮▮▮
Friedrichstr. 158–164, 1080 Berlin. Tel. 2 09 20, fax 229 40 95
370 rooms. Luxurious, all modern amenities.

Hotel Berolina ▮▮
Karl-Marx-Allee 31, 1020 Berlin. Tel. 210 95 41, fax 212 34 09
340 rooms. Near Alexanderplatz. Two restaurants, terrace, roof garden, conference facilities, sauna.

Hotel Metropol ▮▮▮
Friedrichstr. 150, 1080 Berlin. Tel. 20 30 70, fax 20 30 72 09
300 rooms, refurbished in 1989. Four restaurants, all modern amenities.

Hotel Unter den Linden ▮▮
Unter den Linden, 1080 Berlin. Tel. 220 03 11, fax 229 22 62
310 rooms. Comfortable and attractively furnished.

Palasthotel ▮▮▮
Karl-Liebknecht-Str., 1020 Berlin. Tel. 24 10, fax 212 72 73
600 air-conditioned rooms. Opposite the Berlin Cathedral on the banks of the Spree. All modern amenities.

RECOMMENDED RESTAURANTS

We appreciated the food and service in the restaurants listed below; if you find other places worth recommending we'd be pleased to hear from you.

To give you an idea of price (for a starter, main course and dessert), we have used the following symbols:

‖ below 50 DM   ‖‖ 50–70 DM   ‖‖‖ above 70 DM

Many Berlin restaurants close one or two days a week, around Christmas and New Year and for a few weeks in summer. So once you've made your choice, it's best to call to make sure the restaurant is open.

BERLIN CITY, WEST

Bamberger Reiter ‖‖‖
Regensburger Str. 7, 1000 Berlin 30. Tel. 24 42 82
Closed Sunday, Monday, two weeks in January and three in August. Dinner only. Reservation recommended. A refined approach to Tyrolean cuisine. Wonderful desserts. Friendly service.

Taverna Ta Panta Ri ‖
Düsseldorfer Str. 75, 1000 Berlin 15. Tel. 87 73 46
Greek specialities. Frequented by the after-the-theatre crowd.

Café Einstein ‖
Kurfürstenstr. 58, 1000 Berlin. Tel. 261 50 96
Viennese-style coffee house, literary café.

Café Kranzler ‖‖
Kurfürstendamm 18, 1000 Berlin 15. Tel. 882 69 11
Smart bourgeois atmosphere.

Café Möhring

Kurfürstendamm 234, 1000 Berlin 15. Tel. 882 38 44
Open daily 8 a.m.–10 p.m. An institution.

Florian

Grolmanstr. 52, 1000 Berlin 12. Tel. 313 91 84
Reservation advised. Noisy, intellectual chic. Nüremberg cuisine.

Hardtke

Meinekestr. 27, 1000 Berlin 15. Tel. 881 98 27
Open daily 9 a.m.–1 a.m. Traditional Berlin specialities.

Hecker's Deele

Grolmanstr. 35, 1000 Berlin 12. Tel. 8 89 01
First-class traditional German cuisine. Good service.

Kempinski-Grill

Kurfürstendamm 27, 1000 Berlin 15. Tel. 88 43 40
Luxuriously renovated, famed more for décor than for overrated cuisine.

Strada

Potsdamer Str. 131, 1000 Berlin 30. Tel. 215 93 81
Open daily 10 a.m.–2 a.m. Noisy, friendly atmosphere.

CHARLOTTENBURG

Alt Luxemburg

Pestalozzistr. 70, 1000 Berlin 12. Tel. 323 87 30
Excellent, traditional cuisine in bourgeois décor. Reservation advised.
Open Tuesday to Saturday, 7 p.m.–1 a.m.

Paris-Bar

Kantstr. 152, 1000 Berlin 12. Tel. 313 80 52
Classic German and European cuisine in intellectual/arty atmosphere.

Ristorante Mario

Leibnizstr. 43, 1000 Berlin 12. Tel. 324 35 16
Reservation advised. Closed Saturday. Chic Italian restaurant.

KREUZBERG

Bagdad   ‖
Schlesische Str. 2, 1000 Berlin 61. Tel. 612 69 62
Arab restaurant. Small garden with arbour and goldfish pond. Belly-dancing at the weekend.

Gropius   ‖
Stresemannstr. 100, 1000 Berlin 61. Tel. 262 76 20
In the Martin-Gropius-Bau. Vegetarian and whole-food dishes.

Grossbeerenkeller   ‖
Grossbeerenstr. 90, 1000 Berlin 61. Tel. 251 30 64
Open daily 6 p.m.–2 a.m. German cuisine in an ancient cellar.

Hostaria del Monte Croce   ‖
Mittenwalder Str. 6, 1000 Berlin 61. Tel. 694 39 68
Evenings only, closed Sunday and Monday. Reserve in advance. Copious portions of real Italian food, authentic atmosphere.

Thürnagel   ‖
Gneisenaustr. 57, 1000 Berlin 61. Tel. 691 48 00
Daily 6 p.m.–midnight. Vegetarian restaurant.

BERLIN CITY, EAST

Berliner Kaffeehaus   ‖‖‖
Alexanderplatz 2, 1020 Berlin. Tel. 212 50 41
Coffee house with cosy corners. Dancing Friday and Saturday.

Café Arkade   ‖
Französischestr. 25, 1080 Berlin. Tel. 208 02 73
10 a.m.–midnight. Jugendstil décor; small selection of grilled food.

Fondue   ‖
Poststr. 16, 1000 Berlin. Tel. 21 71 32 96
Reservation advised. Cheese fondue served from 5 p.m.

Ganymed   ‖‖‖
Schiffbauerdamm 5, 1040 Berlin. Tel. 282 95 40
International specialities, candlelight and soft music.

Gastmahl des Meeres ▦▦▦
Spandauerstr. 4, 1020 Berlin. Tel. 212 32 86
Closed third Monday of month. Specializes in fish dishes. Friday and Saturday, dancing in cellar.

Wernesgrüner Bierstuben ▦▦▦
Karl-Liebknecht-Str. 11, 1020 Berlin. Tel. 282 42 68
Rustic atmosphere. Traditional cooking.

FURTHER AFIELD

Aphrodite ▦
Schönhauser Allee 61, 1058 Berlin. Tel. 448 17 09
In Prenzlauer Berg. Evenings only. Closed Sunday and July. Innovative, creative chef. Excellent menu, mediocre wine list.

Blockhaus Nikolskoe ▦▦▦
Nikolskoer Weg, Wannsee, 1000 Berlin 39. Tel. 805 29 14
Closed Thursday. German cuisine in a lovely setting overlooking the Havel and Peacock island.

Fioretto ▦
Oberspreestr. 176, Köpenick, 1170 Berlin. Tel. 657 26 05
The best Italian restaurant in eastern Berlin. Excellent service.

Offenbach-Stuben ▦▦
Stubbenkammerstr. 8, 1058 Berlin. Tel. 448 41 06
In Prenzlauer Berg. Closed Sunday and Monday. Reservation advised. Theatrical décor, colourful, sometimes eccentric clientele.

Rockendorf's Restaurant ▦▦▦
Düsterhauptstr. 1, 1000 Berlin 28. Tel. 402 30 99
Berlin's top restaurant, in Waidmannslust. Elegant atmosphere, Jugendstil décor. Reservation essential. Closed three weeks in summer, two weeks at Christmas, Sunday and Monday.

Udagawa ▦▦
Feuerbachstr. 24, Steglitz, 1000 Berlin 41. Tel. 792 23 73
Closed Tuesday. Excellent Japanese cuisine. Reservation essential.

Jewish Museum

(Stresemannstrasse 110, closed Monday.) Awaiting a new building adjoining the Berlin Museum, memorabilia of the city's once flourishing Jewish community are presented in the **Jüdische Abteilung** (Jewish Department) of the Martin-Gropius-Bau. Without ignoring the community's tragic end, the museum emphasizes its positive social, cultural, even sporting role in the local and national life. Exhibits include paintings and sculptures of prominent Jewish figures in Berlin's artistic and social life, documents of the literary salons, photos and ritual artefacts from the synagogues.

Museum für Verkehr und Technik

(Trebbiner Strasse 9, closed Monday.) Built over the railway goods yards of the old Anhalter Bahnhof (see p. 42), the Transport and Technology Museum is devoted not only to rail traffic, but also to aircraft, automobiles and shipping, as well as the technology of communications, printing, medicine and textiles. Visitors are encouraged to manipulate various machines and participate in scientific experiments.

Charlottenburg

The museums in and around the palace are due for a major shake-up, the Egyptian and classical antiquities likely to join the treasures of the Pergamon Museum in eastern Berlin and the Galerie der Romantik destined either for the Tiergarten or the Museumsinsel. The addresses given here apply to the foreseeable future.

Ägyptisches Museum

(Schloss Strasse 70, closed Friday.) The museum boasts one of the greatest collections of Egyptian art outside Egypt itself. It covers 3,000 years of sculpture, pyramid fragments and hieroglyphic tablets. Among recent acquisitions is the monumental **Kalabsha Gate** of 20 B.C., saved from the waters of the Aswan Dam in the 1960s. The carved relief shows Roman Emperor Augustus as an Egyptian Pharaoh.

The most famous piece is undoubtedly the beautiful head of **Queen Nefertiti** (1340 B.C.), consort of Akhenaton. The Germans acquired it by pure luck. It was found in the ancient capital of Tel-el-Amarna just before the outbreak of war in 1914. French archaeologists sharing the dig with the

Germans showed no interest in what they called "a very medio-cre plaster block". Back in Berlin, the plaster was chipped away to reveal the delicate features of Nefertiti, a name meaning "the lovely woman has arrived".

Egyptologists believe the reason she has only one eye is that the head was merely a working model abandoned in a sculptor's workshop when Tutankhamon, successor to Akhenaton, moved his capital to Thebes.

Look out, too, for the many smaller gems in the collection, notably a charming **Married Couple** (2400 B.C.) and the **Ship of Mentuhotep** of 1900 B.C., meticulously carved in wood.

Antikenmuseum

(Schloss-Strasse 1.) This twin museum to the Ägyptisches houses Greek and Roman an-tiquities. Highlights are fine Minoan figurines from Crete, bronzes from Sparta, Samos and Dodona, red-figured Attic vases and a substantial collec-tion of Greek and Etruscan gold ornaments.

Galerie der Romantik

(Schloss Charlottenburg, East Wing; closed Monday.) The palace provides an admirable setting for works by 19th-century Romantic painters Philipp Otto Runge, Friedrich Overbeck, Carl Blechen and Carl Spitzweg. Thieves have deprived the collection, it is hoped temporarily, of Spitz-weg's celebrated *Love Letter* and *The Poor Poet*. Above all, the gallery boasts Germany's most comprehensive collection of works by **Caspar David Friedrich.** Among his mystic land- and seascapes, look for *Abtei im Eichwald* (Abbey in the Woods, 1809), *Der Mönch am Meer* (The Monk by the Sea, 1810) and *Der einsame Baum* (The Lonely Tree, 1822).

Dahlem

The museums of the Prussian State art collections, notably European painting and sculp-ture, are located between Arnimallee and Lansstrasse near Dahlem-Dorf U-Bahn station south-west of Berlin. Dahlem also groups the museums of ethnography (noted for its pre-Columbian collection), Indian, Oriental and Islamic Art. These

Life in the 1920s was typified by the stark realism of Otto Dix, who painted this portrait of his art dealer.

will take over the entire Dahlem installations when the European collections are moved to the Tiergarten's Kulturforum and in part to the Museuminsel in eastern Berlin.

Brücke Museum

(Bussardsteig 9, closed Tuesday.) The museum was created in 1967 thanks to a legacy of Karl Schmidt-Rottluff, member of the Expressionist group *Die Brücke* (The Bridge) that worked in Dresden from 1905 to 1913. His own bold paintings hang beside the searing works of fellow painters Ernst Ludwig Kirchner, Erich Heckel, Max Pechstein and Emil Nolde. Inspired in part by van Gogh, Gauguin and Cézanne, the canvases are a robust reaction to the aesthetic delicacies of Jugendstil.

Gemäldegalerie

(Arnimallee 23, closed Monday.) The collection of European art from the 13th to the 18th centuries ranks among the most important in the world. We present here the highlights.

Italian: Giotto *Death of Mary* (1310); Simone Martini *Entombment of Christ* (1340); Pollaiuolo *Portrait of a Young Woman* (1465); Botticelli *Mary Enthroned* (1484); Giovanni Bellini *Christ Dead, Supported by Two Angels* (1485); Raphael *Madonna Terranuova* (1505); Giorgione *Portrait of a Young Man* (1506); Caravaggio *Amor Vincit Omnia* (1602).

German: Konrad Witz *The Queen of Sheba* (1437); Martin Schongauer *Birth of Christ* (1480); Albrecht Altdorfer *Resting on the Flight to Egypt* (1510); Hans Baldung Grien *Crucifixion* (1512); Albrecht Dürer *Hieronymus Holschuher* (1526); Lucas Cranach *Fountain of Youth* (1546).

Dutch and Flemish: Jan van Eyck *Mary in the Church* (1425); Rogier van der Weyden *St. John Altar* (1450); Hugo van der Goes *Adoration of the Magi* (1470); Pieter Brueghel *Netherlandish Proverbs* (1559); Rubens *St. Sebastian* (1618); van Dyck *Genoese Couple* (1626); Rembrandt *Parable of the Rich Man* (1627); Vermeer *Young Lady with Pearl Necklace* (1665).

French: Georges de La Tour *Peasant Couple Eating* (1620); Poussin *St. Matthew* (1640); Watteau *French Comedy and Italian Comedy* (1716).

Spanish: Velázquez *Portrait of a Lady* (1633); Zurbarán *Don Alonso Verdugo* (1635); Murillo *Baptism of Christ* (1655).

English: Sir Joshua Reynolds

George Clive and his Family (1766); Thomas Gainsborough *The Marsham Children* (1787).

Drawings and prints in the excellent Engravings Department *(Kupferstichkabinett)* range from illuminated manuscripts of the 14th century to modern woodcuts by Expressionist Erich Heckel and lithographs by Willem de Kooning. There are outstanding works by Dürer, Botticelli and Rembrandt.

The **Sculpture Gallery**, also Arnimallee 23, has a magnificent collection of Romanesque and Gothic works from Saxony, Bavaria and the Rhineland and major pieces by Tilman Riemenschneider and Martin Zürn. Italian sculptors represented here include Donatello, Cosimo Tura and Sansovino.

Museumsinsel

The main cluster of museums in eastern Berlin stands on an island just across from Marx-Engels-Platz in a fork of the Spree.

Bodemuseum

(Entrance on Monbijoubrücke, closed Monday and Tuesday.) The museum groups Egyptian, Early Christian, Byzantine and European art. In the **Egyptian collection** is the unfinished sandstone head of a queen (14th century B.C.). She is probably Nefertiti, bringing a complement of delicate grace and serenity to the beauty of the painted head in the Charlottenburg museum.

In the **Early Christian and Byzantine** department, look out for a 6th-century **Ravenna mosaic** from the church of San Michele, depicting Jesus as a young teacher and later, bearded, at the Day of Judgment.

Outstanding in the **sculpture department** are works by Luca and Giovanni della Robbia, Tilman Riemenschneider and Andreas Schlüter.

Because American troops retrieved the Berlin art treasures stored in Thuringia, most of the best ended up in Dahlem rather than on the Museumsinsel. But the Bode's **European paintings** do include notable works by Lucas Cranach, Adam Elsheimer, Jan van Goyen, Jakob van Ruisdael, Abraham Bloemaert and Nicolas Poussin.

Nationalgalerie

(Bodestrasse 1, closed Monday and Tuesday.) Although its collection was depleted by Hitler's assault on "Degenerate Art" and the ravages of war, the museum has some interesting **German works** of the 19th and

20th centuries: Carl Blechen, Ferdinand Georg Waldmüller, Max Slevogt and Max Liebermann (*The Flax Workers* and portraits of Wilhelm von Bode and Richard Strauss). Adolph von Menzel's *Eisenwalzwerk* (The Iron Foundry, 1875) is a striking portrayal of industrial labour. Oscar Kokoschka's *Pariser Platz* (1926) recalls the bustle that surrounded Brandenburg Gate in the turbulent Twenties. The Expressionist *Brücke* school is present with works by Emil Nolde, Karl Schmidt-Rottluff, Erich Heckel and Ernst Ludwig Kirchner. Later Expressionists include Otto Dix and Lovis Corinth.

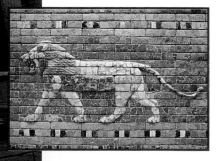

Pergamon Museum's gateway to an ancient Roman market, and a detail from processional street in Babylon.

The small collection of **European painting** includes works by Goya, Courbet, Degas and Cézanne. Among the **sculpture,** notice Johann Gottfried Schadow's charming double statue of the Prussian princesses Luise and Friederike and also works by Auguste Rodin, Georg Kolbe and Ernst Barlach.

Pergamonmuseum

(Kupfergraben, closed Monday and Tuesday.) Housing many magnificent works of classical antiquity, the Near East, Islam and the Orient, the museum is named after its most prized possession: the gigantic **Pergamon Altar** (2nd century B.C.). This masterpiece of Hellenistic art comes from what is now Bergama, near the west coast of Turkey. The massive colonnaded altar dedicated to Zeus and Athena has been constructed to fill one hall of the museum. A frieze more than 2 m. (7 ft.) high extends along the altar's base, relating the tortured struggle of the Greek gods with the giants.

Equally impressive is the **Babylonian Processional Street** (604–562 B.C.), built by King Nebuchadnezzar II. Lions sculpted in relief stride along the street's blue and ochre tiled walls towards Ishtar Gate. Bulls and dragons decorate the gate, also in blue and ochre tile. The museum's scale model shows how the processional street continued through the gate, on the edge of the city of Babylon, to a house set aside for New Year festivities.

A third great treasure is the Roman **Market gate of Miletus**, from Greek Asia Minor (A.D. 165). Its mundane name belies the elaborately pedimented monument, both gateway and shopping complex.

The **Islamic Museum** in the Pergamon's south wing exhibits the grand façade of the 8th-century **Palace of Mshatta** (from modern Jordan). It is embellished with intricately

---

GIFT HUNTING IN MUSEUMS

Museum shops are a good place to find art posters, lithographs and high-quality reproductions. In museums of classical antiquity like the Ägyptisches, Antiken- and Pergamon museums, you can get excellent copies of Greek vases or ancient sculpture in bronze, plaster or resin. Museum shops also offer a certain guarantee of quality for genuine artisan products—textiles, pottery, pewter, decorative candles and woodcarving.

incised or perforated animal or plant motifs. A German art historian rescued this tour de force of early Islamic decoration at the beginning of the 20th century by dissuading the Sultan of Turkey from using it as building material for a railway to Mecca. Among the other precious exhibits is an exquisite 14th-century **Spanish synagogue carpet** decorated with the sacred scrolls of the Hebrew Torah (Law). There are also some fine Indian **Mogul miniatures**.

Märkisches Museum

(Am Köllnischen Park 5, closed Monday and Tuesday.) Located near Inselbrücke on the south bank of the Spree, the museum derives its name from the *Mark* (territory) of Brandenburg which surrounds Berlin. It has a delightful collection of Berliniana: the first bicycles, sewing machines, telephones—and the 1881 telephone directory with all of 41 names in it—a 19th-century worker's kitchen, and a model of the infamous tenements that nurtured unrest prior to the 1848 revolution. The exhibits are generally an interesting proletarian counterpart to the predominantly bourgeois displays of the Berlin Museum in Kreuzberg (see p. 64). A special section is given over to Berlin's great theatre history, highlighting the productions of Max Reinhardt and the works of Bertolt Brecht. The museum's most striking exhibit is one of the original sculpted horse's heads from the Quadriga on Brandenburg Gate.

Nikolaiviertel

This neighbourhood has been reconstructed and preserved as an extension of the Märkisches Museum, to present a composite picture of city life from the Middle Ages to the 19th century. The **Nikolaikirche** shows the history of the Berlin and Cölln townships from the 13th–17th centuries, including Gothic, Renaissance and Baroque church sculpture; craftwork is presented in reconstructed workshops with all the tools of the trade in the Berliner Handwerksmuseum (Mühlendamm 5); Baroque and Biedermeier paintings are displayed in the Ephraimpalais (Poststrasse 16). In the **Knoblauchhaus** (Poststrasse 23), a picture of the Berlin bourgeoisie can be formed through the life of the Knoblauch family from an 18th-century manufacturer of pins and needles to prosperous architects, brewers and municipal politicians.

EXCURSIONS

Since the disappearance of the Wall, the idea of an excursion outside the city limits has become an adventure for Berliners themselves that will not quickly lose its novelty. People are rediscovering Berlin's hinterland. The young are exploring places of which grandparents talked nostalgically or showed faded photos from their own childhood. We have limited our suggestions here to the city's nearby surroundings, all reachable on an easy day-trip. This will enable you to return to your accommodation in Berlin, as hotel facilities outside the city are likely to remain difficult for the immediate future. For those wishing to explore further afield, we recommend the chapter on Eastern Germany in the Berlitz Blueprint Guide to Germany.

The gilded teahouse in Potsdam indulged an 18th-century taste for chinoiserie.

BRANDENBURG

The state surrounding but excluding Berlin became the Hohenzollerns' power base in the 15th century, gradually incorporating the Prussian territories until being absorbed in the new kingdom of Prussia in 1701. The region east to Frankfurt an der Oder at the Polish border is largely industrial. But pretty forests and lakes characterize the area west of Berlin around Potsdam, the royal capital, and the ancient bishopric of Brandenburg which gave the state its name.

Potsdam

In the eyes of Europe, Potsdam was Prussia. Soldier King Friedrich Wilhelm I laid out parade grounds here for his beloved Prussian infantry to goose-step to the forefront of European armies. His son, Frederick the Great, refined the image by attracting to his

Sanssouci palace the cream of Europe's artists and intellectuals. Goebbels plumped for Potsdam's militarist tradition for the Führer's blessing by Field Marshal Hindenburg in the Garnisonskirche (Garrison Church). And Potsdam witnessed the end of it all when the victorious Allies met here in 1945 to carve up the Reich.

The town today is a green and pleasant place of parks and woodland around the palaces west of the city centre and north along the lake of Heiliger See—great places for a picnic.

Frederick the Great's **Schloss Sanssouci** was designed by Georg von Knobelsdorff in 1745 from the king's own sketches. Frederick wanted a place where he could forget the affairs of state and pursue his passion for philosophy and the arts without worry—*sans souci*. The result is a graceful Rococo edifice perfectly integrated with its terraced gardens. In the palace's interior, see the handsome cedar-panelled library in the east wing's rotunda. Next to the king's study and bedroom is a splendid Concert Room with paintings by Antoine Pesne. In the west wing is Voltaire's study, where the French writer served as writer-in-residence from 1750 to 1753.

The royal **Bildergalerie** (Picture Gallery) east of the palace displays works by Flemish and Italian masters, notably Caravaggio *Doubting Thomas;* Guido Reni *Death of Cleopatra;* Rubens *Coronation of Diana;* and van Dyck *Adoration of the Shepherds.*

South-west of the terraced gardens and fountain, take a look at Frederick's **Chinesisches Teehaus**, a pavilion with gilded palm trees for columns and a pagoda-style roof topped by a gilded mandarin. Some fine Chinese porcelain is displayed inside.

Beside the lake north of the city centre is a pleasant English-style park, **Neuer Garten**, landscaped in 1824 by Peter Joseph Lenné. It provides an apt setting for **Schloss Cecilienhof**, the ivy-covered, half-timbered pastiche of an English country manor. Built in 1916 for Crown Prince Wilhelm and his wife Cecilie, this architectural oddity is crowned with no less than 55 chimneys of which only three actually work. Unlike a real English country house, it has excellent central heating.

Winston Churchill (and then Clement Attlee), Harry Truman and Joseph Stalin met here in July 1945 to draw up the Potsdam Agreement that fixed the division of Germany for the next 45 years. Since this provided the German Democratic Republic's raison d'être, the conference room and delegation suites were preserved with the summit meeting's original tables, desks and national flags. One of the documents exhibited lists John Fitzgerald Kennedy among the accredited press photographers.

Outside the palace parks, the war spared little of old Potsdam, but among the restored buildings see the handsome Baroque **Oberrechnungs-kammer** (Accounting House) dating from the 18th century, Yorkstrasse 19. Nearby is Karl Friedrich Schinkel's massive Palladian-style neoclassical **Nikolaikirche**. The elegant **Marstall** (Royal Stables) was redesigned by Knobelsdorff in 1746; its equestrian sculpture over the porticos is by Friedrich Christian Glume, who did much of the statuary for Sanssouci. The stables now house a Film Museum, recalling Berlin's golden era of film-making in the 20s when the studios in the Potsdam suburb of Babelsberg were more than a match for Hollywood.

On the outskirts of Babelsberg south of the Havel river, Albert-Einstein-Strasse climbs Telegrafenberg to the bizarre white **Einsteinturm** built in 1921 as an astrophysics observatory by Expressionist architect Erich Mendelsohn. Set in a lovely park, this unique structure has the various nautical forms of a rudder, stern and funnel, and the interior of the "forward" lab is laid out like a captain's bridge. The great scientist only attended a few committee meetings there, but was present at a memorable technical demonstration of his theory of relativity in the tower, 20 m. (66 ft.) high. For want of a statue to the great man, observatory staff have placed in the entrance hall as a splendidly atrocious visual pun a simple small stone—*Ein Stein*. A few kilometres further south in the pretty lakeshore village of Caputh is **Einstein's home,** Am Wald 7, from which he emigrated to America in 1933.

All around Potsdam, on the **Templiner lake** and in the forests and parks of Charlottenhof, Petzow and Werder, you will find plenty of opportunities for picnics, rambling and boating.

Brandenburg Town

On the Havel river about 40 km. (25 mi.) west of Potsdam on Highway 1, the town is a good base for visiting the surrounding lakes—Beetz See, known for its regattas, and Plauer See and Breitlingsee for swimming. The bishopric converted to Protestantism in 1567, but the Romanesque-Gothic cathedral, on an island in the river, has retained much of its interior ornament. Notice the 13th-century stained glass, some finely sculpted capitals, and above all, the striking *Coronation of Mary* painted for the 14th-century Bohemian Altar.

South of the cathedral island, in the Neustadt district, visit the 15th-century **Katharinen-**

Offering a hint of the open sea when Berlin was enclosed in its western sector, the Havel river is now a marina for all.

kirche to see the admirable Flamboyant Gothic gables and rose windows of the Corpus Christi chapel *(Fronleichnamskapelle)*.

In the Altstadt district west of the cathedral, the dignified 15th-century step-gabled brick **town hall** has a lofty clock tower and Gothic porch with a rather gloomy-looking statue of Charlemagne's worthy knight Roland, symbol of civic freedom, in front.

Some 20 km. (12 mi.) southeast of town is the largely 13th-century **Lehnin Monastery** (restored in 1877). The brick ensemble of church, granary, abbot's house and cloisters is a fine example of late-Romanesque and Gothic, a style brought here by Cistercian monks from northern France.

WHAT TO DO

In this liveliest of German cities, there is no lack of activities when your sightseeing day is done. Whatever the vagaries of world politics, Berlin has never relinquished its role as national capital in the realm of the performing arts, of shopping for luxury goods, high and low fashion in chic boutiques or colourful flea markets, or of sport with the first-class facilities of its exceptional wide open spaces.

ENTERTAINMENT

Berliners are the most assiduous concert- and theatre-goers in Europe, and you have to plan ahead if you want good tickets for the "main events". Ask your travel agency or the German national tourist office for details of upcoming music and

Transvestites continue the unholy tradition of Berlin nightclubs.

theatre programmes, and book in advance where possible. However, good hotels will always help you find seats on the spot if you are prepared to pay a little extra. The weekly newspaper *Die Zeit*, on sale outside Germany, has programmes of theatre, concerts—and art exhibitions. In addition to the tourist office's *Berlin Programm*, there are no less than three bright city-magazines, *tip, zitty* and *tempo*, similar to London's *Time Out*, giving full details and reviews.

Music

Symphonic music is at the very centre of the city's artistic life. The town boasts three of the world's finest orchestras. The Berlin Philharmonic achieved its post-war glory under the late Herbert von Karajan, but has more than maintained its position under his successors. Its home is the Philharmonie (see p. 39) where the audience surrounds the orchestra on all sides in a setting of matchless acoustics. The highly rated Radio Symphony Orchestra also performs there in addition to its broadcasting hall in the Haus des Rundfunks (Masurenallee 8–10). The Berlin Symphony Orchestra can be heard in the Apollo-Saal of the Deutsche Staatsoper on Unter den Linden, and in Schinkel's magnificently restored Schauspielhaus, its interior converted from theatre to concert hall.

Chamber music and *Lieder* (song) recitals take place in the Kammermusiksaal at the rear of the Philharmonie, in the Ephraimpalais (Nikolaiviertel), the Akademie der Künste (Hansaviertel) and the Hochschule der Künste, Hardenbergstrasse 33.

Schloss Charlottenburg provides a charming decor for summer music festivals, while the city's churches, especially the Kaiser Wilhelm and Kaiser Friedrich memorial churches, make an appropriate setting for oratorios, requiems and other religious works.

Opera lovers are well served by the Deutsche Oper in the Bismarckstrasse, the Deutsche Staatsoper on Unter den Linden and the Komische Oper in Behrenstrasse.

Jazz and **rock** are performed in big halls like the Philharmonie, Deutschlandhalle, Neue Friedrichstadtpalast, Eissporthalle and Metropol-Musikpalast or in dozens of small *Musikkneipen* (music-bars) and cafés, served live with your beer, wine or coffee.

Theatre

Berlin is one of the most exciting and innovative theatre towns in the world, so that even without a great command of the German language any enthusiastic playgoer can enjoy some stirring performances. It is the German custom for the major theatres, like the opera, to maintain several productions in repertory, so that in any one week you get a chance to see the same troupe perform contemporary or classical drama.

The Schiller-Theatre (Bismarckstrasse 110) is respected for its authoritative productions of the classics—German and international—while its Werkstatt offers "workshop" productions of avant-garde plays. Somewhere between the two is the Schlosspark-Theater (Schloss-Strasse 48), which provides an intimate setting for Molière, Shakespeare and the German classics.

The city's most audacious and versatile repertory is to be found at the Schaubühne (Ku'damm and Lehninerplatz). Its habitually almost brutally uncompromising performances of classical avant-garde and experimental theatre have achieved international renown. The stance is perpetually provocative, delighting in catching German society on the wrong foot, questioning the blessings of German unification, pinpointing the dubious virtues of capitalist freedoms. Whereas this kind of theatre is usually performed on a shoestring budget, the Schaubühne has at its disposal stage machinery that is among the most elaborate and sophisticated in the world.

But that more modest vanguard is very present, too, in a whole host of fringe groups (*freie Gruppen*) that come and go with the ephemeral brilliance of shooting stars. To distinguish themselves from the meretricious commercial theatre, they sport such forbidding names as Theatermanufaktur (Hallesches Ufer 61), Atelier Internationale Kunst (Dahlmannstrasse 11) or Transformtheater (Hasenheide 54). And the meretricious commercial theatre is not to be sneezed at, either. For the middle-brow equivalents of Broadway or Shaftesbury Avenue musicals, comedies and operettas, try the very professional Theater am Kurfürstendamm (No. 209), the Komödie (Ku'damm 206), the Renaissance-Theater (Hardenbergstrasse 6) and the highly popular Theater des Westens (Kantstrasse 12).

Eastern Berlin has also contributed to the ongoing theatre tradition, thanks largely to the efforts of its best-known dramatist, Bert Brecht, who founded the world-famous Berliner Ensemble (Bertolt-Brecht-Platz). Like the Royal Shakespeare in England, the master's plays dominate the repertory, which does, however, expand to other, mostly modern classics. Contemporary plays are performed at the Maxim-Gorki-Theater (Am Festungsgraben 2) and the classics at the Deutsches Theater (Schumannstrasse 13a), former home of the great Max Reinhardt. The Metropol-Theater (Friedrichstrasse 101) proposes lighter entertainment, while the Neue Friedrichstadt-Palast (also on Friedrichstrasse) has replaced since 1985 the historic but structurally fragile home of Berlin variety shows.

Another long-standing Berlin tradition, at its heyday in the 1920s, **satirical cabaret** has always, by its very nature, had to struggle for its existence. But Berlin, also by its very nature, has always seemed to provide the necessary raw material, a perennially turbulent political and social history to which reunification is unlikely to put a stop. Three survivors among the myriad fly-by-nights are Die Stachelschweine (The Porcupines, Europa-Center) re-emerging from a long period of complacency, Die Wühlmäuse (The Voles, Nürnberger Strasse 33) and, from a psychologically more sensitive point of view in *eastern* Berlin, Die Distel (The Thistle, Friedrichstrasse 101).

Nightclubs range from the delightfully garish girlie show to the conventional discotheque. In between are the more interesting transvestite shows, "naughty", often very witty and rarely more than mildly offensive—who would want to see a transvestite show that was not offensive at all? They provide an amusing link with Berlin's past through impersonations of Marlene Dietrich, Zarah Leander and other "inimitables".

Older folk—and a few younger gigolos to keep them happy—congregate at the **ballroom dances** held in the Tanzpalast, Café des Westens, Café Keese or Café Huthmacher. Gamblers who do not need a glamorous Monte Carlo setting will find roulette, blackjack and baccarat at the very modern **casino** *(Spielbank)* in the Europa-Center and in some of the big hotels in eastern Berlin.

SPORTS

Thanks to the many lakes and rivers, the city does not lack for **swimming** opportunities. There are some 20 beaches, most of them as pleasantly sandy as on the Mediterranean. Continuing the old Prussian devotion to physical culture, a few of the beaches are reserved for nude bathing—FKK, as you may see it signposted in German. The most popular of these are the Bullenwinkel on the Grunewaldsee and—closer to the city centre—Strandbad Halensee on the Teufelssee. If you would rather wear a swimsuit, try the lovely beaches of the Wannsee, Glienicker See, the Havel, the less crowded Grosser Müggelsee in eastern Berlin and Templiner See out at Potsdam.

Bathing beauties on Wannsee's beaches keep all their clothes around them, just in case.

Throughout the city there are open-air and indoor swimming pools. Berlin's Luft und Badeparadies (*Blub* for short) in Buschkrugallee, Neukölln, offers both indoor and outdoor pools, plus water slides, a cascade, solarium and restaurants.

At Berlin's lakes, you can rent equipment for almost all the **water sports**—sailing, water-skiing, canoeing, rowing and wind-surfing.

If you feel like **fishing**, get yourself a very good barbecued supper of whitefish, perch, pike or eel on the Havel, Müggelsee and the Glienicker See. The Berlin tourist information centre will give you details about a licence and boat-hire.

The best trails for **horse riding** are in the Grunewald. Hire a mount at Onkel Toms Hütte, Zehlendorf. Children can ride ponies in Wittenau and Marienfelde.

Golf enthusiasts can get a game in at the Wannsee Club, Stölpchenweg. Your own home club membership can usually gain you entrance.

Boris Becker and Steffi Graf have made **tennis** a favourite national sport, and **squash** is also catching on fast. Both are well served, so to speak, at courts citywide, notably Paulsborner Strasse (near the Ku'damm) and Angerburger Allee (near Heerstrasse).

One sport you might not have expected to practice in Berlin is **hang-gliding**, but it is possible to float off the Teufelsberg. Which is where you can also do a little **skiing** and **toboganing** in winter.

Try **roller skating** in summer or **ice skating** in winter at the rink in Wilmersdorf (Fritz-Wildungs-Strasse). In the Tiergarten, roller skaters and **joggers** maintain a relationship of mutual disrespect. The most pleasant defence against the natural aggressivity of the city's **bicycle** riders is to rent one yourself at the Fahrradbüro Berlin, Hauptstrasse 146.

Spectator sports

With the withdrawal of American troops from Berlin, the only kind of **football** you are likely to see is of the soccer variety. Watch the local professional teams at the Olympic Stadium and the Friedrich-Ludwig-Jahn-Sportpark.

You can see **ice hockey** at the Eissporthalle and international **rowing** regattas on the Hohenzollern canal. International **tennis** tournaments are held at the Rot-Weiss club. **Horse racing** fans can see trotting (*Trabrennen*) at Mariendorf.

SHOPPING
Where to Shop

One thing the fall of the Wall did not change overnight—indeed it served only to emphasize it even more—was the role of western Berlin as a big shop window for western consumer society. The "main branch" is undoubtedly still the area on and around the Ku'damm and it will take some time before new construction on Potsdamer Platz or redevelopment of Alexanderplatz will provide any competition.

The easy exchange of goods through the European Common Market and the Germans' own taste for things exotic and foreign mean that you can probably find anything here from practically anywhere in the world. But along with the Germans' high standard of living comes a high price tag on most imported goods, so you are better off buying "Made in Germany".

Fashionable boutiques and big department stores like Wertheim line the Ku'damm itself while the cherished institution of KaDeWe (Kaufhaus des Westens, see p. 36) is situated close by in Tauentzienstrasse. The Europa-Center near the Gedächtniskirche is a multi-storey shopping mall. There are also shopping arcades like Ku'damm-Karree (corner of Uhlandstrasse) and Ku'damm-Eck (corner of Joachimstaler Strasse).

Most shops open around 9 a.m. and close by 6 p.m. They close Saturday afternoons, 1 or 2 p.m., except for the first Saturday of the month.

What to Buy
Antiques

As always a high-risk and high-price business, antiques these days are increasingly an affair in closed circuit among the antique dealers themselves. Any moderately priced Baroque and Rococo furniture or porcelain is probably a copy. You are better advised to concentrate on products of the 19th and early 20th centuries, but genuine Biedermeier, Jugendstil or Art Deco may also be very expensive. Even ponderous pieces from bourgeois homes of the pre-1914 Wilhelminian era have moved out of the domain of High Kitsch.

Gourmet Delicacies

The delicatessens make up attractive gift parcels of sausage, hams and pickles. At the

Konditorei (pastry shops), goodies that travel best are *Lebkuchen* (gingerbread), *Spekulatius* (spiced Christmas cookies) and marzipan in all shapes and sizes, including a Hansel-and-Gretel house that you may never want to eat. KaDeWe's food department on the sixth floor offers 500 different kinds of bread, 1,000 kinds of sausage and 1,500 different cheeses. Berlin has no local wine but plenty of wine-shops to satisfy connoisseurs of the best Rhine, Mosel and Baden-Württemberg vintages.

Kitchen Equipment

The electrical appliances are superbly designed with the streamlined look of the Bauhaus tradition. You will find an endless array of highest-quality kitchen knives. One marvellous horror that belongs more properly in our "Souvenirs and Kitsch" section is a nutcracker in the form of a Prussian army sergeant busting the nut between his jaws.

Music and Precision Instruments

The land of Bach and Beethoven feels it its duty to offer a selection of records second only to that of the United States. If you are in the market for a musical instrument, you will find the finest harmonicas as well as the grandest pianos.

Germany has relinquished its pre-war domination of the camera market to Japan, but artists and spies still lust after the Leica and Minox. Best buys are the telescopes and binoculars. Miniature but powerful binoculars are great aids for your sightseeing, not so much for long-distance viewing outside, but for inside the cathedrals and palaces to get a close-up of remote details.

Porcelain and Linen

The manufacture of tableware and decorative objects continues a great German tradition. Look out for modern Rosenthal and the local KPM, launched by Frederick the Great in the 18th century and continued now by the Staatliche Porzellan Manufaktur with showrooms and shops at Wegelystrasse 1 and Kurfürstendamm 26a. Other celebrated manufacturers represented in Berlin, particularly in antique shops, are Meissen, Nymphenburg of Munich, and Frankenthal.

Flea markets like this can be found in the Tiergarten, on the banks of the Landwehr canal, and near Pankow town hall.

Bed and table linens here are of the finest old-fashioned quality. The duck- or goose-down *Federbett* (duvet) is a lifetime investment. In addition to the warm-as-toast winter model, look out for the light-weight for summer.

Souvenirs and Kitsch

The Germans just cannot help making even their most dreadful souvenirs solid enough to last forever, so choose carefully or be prepared to throw them away when people stop laughing.

. Some of the best or worst ideas, according to your taste: giant earthenware or porcelain beer mugs, with or without lid, hats with partridge feathers or shaving brushes on the brim or clay pipes with bowl in the form of a lady's bare bottom.

In the realm of High Kitsch, with price tag to match, collectors' items wander ambivalently between the comic and the hideous. Spiked *Pickelhaube* helmets from Kaiser Wilhelm's army are old enough now to be quite charming. But there is also a fascination with what might be dubbed collectively as *Totalitariana*—uniforms and insignia of the Nazi era and, since November 1989, the East German and Soviet armies. You may find the most appropriate commentary in World War II *Wehrmacht* helmets that sometimes turn up, enamelled, as converted chamber pots.

A warning: just as the number of church relics of the True Cross could make a dozen crosses, so there are now in circulation enough pieces of the Berlin Wall "certified genuine" to divide in two the cities of Munich, Hamburg, Frankfurt and Stuttgart, too.

Toys

The great talents the Germans bring to their manufacturing industries find a natural outlet for children—and parents—in toys of every imaginable kind. The electric trains are the world's best. Others swear by the model aircraft, boats and spaceships. There are construction kits for building your own Baroque palace or medieval castle. Berlin specializes in tin soldiers to refight old battles, not excluding World War II, though here the battles tend to be in the air with Stukas and Messerschmidts against Spitfires and Dakotas.

If this makes German toy shops sound like an exclusively boys' world, the dolls in traditional costume and superb teddies and other cuddly creatures more than redress the balance. To spoil the kid-that-has-everything, you can also find exquisite dolls' tea services in copies of KPM, Meissen, Frankenthal and Nymphenburger porcelain. The ultimate posh toy for the truly sophisticated toddler is a little box of Bauhaus building blocks to be found at major modern-art museum shops.

Turkish Products

The *Gastarbeiter* colony, concentrated mainly in Kreuzberg and Neukölln, has created its own Turkish bazaar *(Türkischer Wochenmarkt)* on the Landwehr canal's Maybachufer. You can buy exotic foods, spices and Turkish utensils Tuesday and Friday afternoons.

CALENDAR OF EVENTS

Since reunification, the city's arts calendar is undergoing the same "revolution" as the rest of the town. Not all events mentioned below are held every year, but the list gives an idea of what to look out for.

January	*Berliner Musiktage*, a three-week contemporary music festival.
February/March	Even Protestant Berlin has a Carnival of banquets, balls and processions. The International Film Festival rivals Cannes and Venice.
April	*Berliner Kunsttage*, two weeks of art exhibitions and "happenings".
May	*Theatertreffen*, German-language theatre festival from all over Germany, Austria and Switzerland.
June	*Horizonte*, festival of music from Asia, Africa and Latin America.
July/August	Summer Music Festival, open-air folk, rock and jazz concerts, evening performances on floodlit Ku'damm.
September/ October	*Berliner Festwochen,* major international festival of opera, theatre, music and art.
October/November	Jazz Festival, mainstream and avant-garde.
December	*Weihnachtsmarkt,* traditional Berlin Christmas market.

EATING OUT

Good news: there is a new German cuisine. Enduring prosperity and constant travel to western Europe and further afield to the old civilizations of Asia have created a demand for greater culinary refinement. Good old German dishes are not being replaced by French, Italian, Japanese or Chinese imitations. But increasingly, they are cooked with a new delicacy and imagination. One thing has not changed: generous portions for robust appetites. You will not starve.

Meal Times

Lunch (*Mittagessen*) is usually served from 11.30 a.m. to 2 p.m., dinner (*Abendessen*) from 6.30 to 9.30 p.m. (later in large establishments). Most Germans like to eat their main meal in the middle of the day.

Café Möhring has one of the few Jugendstil façades to survive on the Ku'damm.

They generally prefer a light supper (*Abendbrot*, "evening bread"), consisting of cold meats and cheeses with the possible addition of a salad.

Where to Eat

The range is from high-class *Restaurant* and bourgeois *Gaststätte* via the chic and sometimes arty *Bistro*—the French word has stuck—to the popular *Kneipe*, originally student slang for any corner bar or tavern where you can have a drink and a snack heavy enough to call a meal.

More and more, influenced by Mediterranean travel, all these places spill out onto the streets and squares for open-air meals as soon as the weather is warm enough, notably on the Ku'damm, Potsdamer Strasse and Unter den Linden and around Savignyplatz.

Call them *Bräuhaus* (literally brewery) or *Bierkeller*, the old beer-halls are still going strong, becoming *Biergarten* in the parks—oom-pah-pah bands and all.

The *Konditorei* (café-cum-pastry shop) is in a separate category all its own. In this bourgeois fairyland, armed with a newspaper attached to a rod, you can stuff yourself with pastry, ice cream, coffee, tea, hot chocolate and fruit juices, even a good selection of wines. Most also offer a few egg dishes, light snacks and salads. The clientele varies in age but everybody looks 55. They hold court most royally at Cafés Kranzler and Möhring on the Ku'damm and the Operncafé on Unter den Linden. A more youthful outgrowth is the *Frühstückskneipe*, a café specializing in breakfast, sometimes starting at 3 a.m. and going on all day long.

Breakfast

Berliners start the day with a meal that is somewhat more substantial than the typical "continental" breakfast. The distinctive touch is the selection of cold meats—ham, salami and liver sausage (*Leberwurst*)—and cheese served with the bread. Not just one kind of bread, but white with sesame or poppy seeds, brown rye with caraway seeds, rich black *Pumpernickel* or crisp wafer-thin *Knäckebrot*. If you like boiled eggs, try *Eier im Glas*, two four-minute eggs served whole, already shelled, in a glass dish. Gone the problem of whether to smash or guillotine the top. And with all that, tea, hot chocolate or coffee that is stronger than the Anglo-American brew, but weaker than French or Italian.

TABLE MANNERS

On one or two of the long tables in the beer halls or other big restaurants, you will occasionally see a sign proclaiming *Stammtisch*—table for regulars. The custom dates back to the medieval craft guilds, and today the tables are kept for firms, social clubs or big families. It is otherwise customary for strangers to sit together, usually after a polite query as to whether one of the six or seven empty places is *"frei"*. As they sit down they wish each other *"Mahlzeit"* or *"Guten Appetit"*.

It may come as a surprise that each bread roll (*Brötchen* or *Semmel*) is charged separately; you are expected to keep a count of how many you eat.

In the smarter establishments, casual elegance has usually replaced the old formality of ties for men and skirts for women.

Soups and Starters

In Berlin, you can sample all the traditional German soups. *Leberknödelsuppe* comes with spicy dumplings of flour, breadcrumbs, ox liver, onions, marjoram and garlic. At its best, *Kartoffelsuppe* combines potato, celery, leeks and parsnips, while *Bohnensuppe* is a hearty concoction of different varieties of beans. But the city's favourite is plain old lentil soup *(Linsensuppe),* best with pieces of sausage in it.

Typical starters include *Hackepeter,* the German version of steak tartare, and *Soleier,* eggs pickled in brine *(Sole),* then peeled, halved and seasoned with salt, pepper, paprika, vinegar and oil. They are usually eaten with the ubiquitous Berlin mustard—*Mostrich.*

Main Dishes

Fish comes fresh from the Havel. Try specialities like *Havelaal grün,* eel boiled in a dill sauce, or *Havelzander,* pike-perch served with *Salzkartoffeln,* simple but surprisingly tasty boiled potatoes. Potatoes are something of a Berlin obsession. A local curiosity, still found in the old neighbourhoods, is the potato shop selling nothing but eight or more different varieties. One of the city's great gourmet delights is the *Kartoffelpuffer,* a crispy potato pancake.

But the supreme Berlin delicacy is *Eisbein mit Sauerkraut und Erbsenpüree*—pig's knuckle on a purée of peas with Sauerkraut prepared in white wine, juniper berries, caraway seeds and cloves. Plus, as always, a good dollop of mustard. More humble, but just as fine, is *gebratene Leber,* sautéed liver with slices of apple and browned onion rings.

The original recipe for smoked pork chops dubbed *Kasseler Rippen* came not from the town of Kassel but from a Berlin butcher named Herr Kassel. Berlin also claims two world-famous sausages: the giant *Bockwurst,* so named since a local butcher advertised it suspended between the mouths of two goats *(Bock);* and even the Viennese sausage or *Wiener* was invented, they say, in Berlin.

Foreign Restaurants

In a city with so many foreign residents, a great variety of Balkan, Mediterranean and Indo-Pakistani restaurants have sprung up in recent years. Some of the Italian restaurants here are often regarded as the best

outside Italy, particularly in Munich and Berlin. Turkish restaurants take pride of place, but you can compare with Greek establishments and decide who does better what are largely the same dishes.

Snacks

O.K., Berliners do not claim to have invented the hamburger, but they have something they consider to be vastly superior: *Bulette*. This glorified meatball or *Frikadelle*, as it is called outside Berlin, is most often dispensed by mobile stalls that usually stay open till the early hours of the morning—a welcome sight to the cold and hungry night-owl. They also sell *Schaschlik*, *Currywurst* (sausage in a curry sauce) and *Thüringer Rostbratwurst*—German sausage at its most tangy.

Desserts

A popular sweet is *Rote Grütze* (compote of raspberries, cherries and blackcurrants). Otherwise, Berliners happily go along with the national orgy of Konditorei treats like *Schwarz-*

On Nollendorfplatz, far from the sophisticated image of its intellectuals, Berlin café life also has a rougher edge to it.

wälder Kirschtorte, the creamy cherry cake from the Black Forest, and *Apfelstrudel* from Vienna. They are also partial to hazelnut cream cake *(Haselnuss-Sahnetorte)*, cheese cake *(Käsekuchen)*—though you cannot convince Americans it is better than their own—and the Dresden plum-cake *(Pflaumenkuchen)*.

Drinks

Frederick the Great tried to make wine at Potsdam and it was terrible, but Berlin restaurants offer a first-class array of German wines. The red wines cannot compare in quality to the famous whites of the Rhine and Mosel Valleys, but the whole family of German wines is very respectable.

The most highly reputed wines are those of the Rheingau. Among the top labels are Schloss Johannisberger, Hattenheimer, Kloster Eberbacher, Steinberger and Rüdesheimer. Celebrate with the very creditable champagne-like *Sekt*. The best Rhine Valley reds come from Assmannshausen and Ingelheim.

From Rheinhessen, try the popular Liebfraumilch or the great Niersteiner Domtal and Oppenheimer. The Mosel wines, bottled in green glass to distinguish them from the brown Rhine bottles, enjoy their own delicate reputation, the most celebrated being the Bernkasteler, Piesporter, Graacher and Zeltinger.

Berlin's most popular drink remains beer—local Schultheiss and Warburger or the best Dortmund and Bavarian brews. They are served *vom Fass*, on tap, or bottled in several varieties: *Export*, light and smooth; *Pils*, light and strong; and *Bock*, dark and rich (very good with the sausage of the same name).

As a refreshing surprise in summer, try the *Berliner Weisse*, a foaming draught beer served in a huge bowl-like glass with a shot of raspberry syrup or liqueur—or green woodruff syrup *(Waldmeister)*.

Berliners also like the custom of "chasing" the beer with a shot of Schnaps—any hard, clear alcohol made from potato, corn, barley, juniper or other grain or berry that will distill into something to warm the cockles of your heart.

The brandy *(Weinbrand)* is not bad, but the fruit Schnaps distilled from cherries *(Kirschwasser)*, plums *(Zwetschgenwasser)* or raspberries *(Himbeergeist)* are much better.

Whatever your "poison," *Prost!*

BLUEPRINT
FOR A PERFECT TRIP

CONTENTS

AN A–Z SUMMARY
OF PRACTICAL INFORMATION

Listed after many entries is the appropriate German translation, usually in the singular, plus a number of phrases that should be of help if you require assistance.

(W) and (E) after certain telephone numbers refer to old West and East Berlin: the telecommunications system has not yet been unified. Germans themselves refer to West and East as *West* and *Ost,* respectively.

ACCOMMODATION. See also CAMPING and YOUTH HOSTELS. The Berlin tourist office *(Verkehrsamt Berlin)* publishes a free multilingual list with full details of amenities and prices of accommodation in the city. They also provide a booking service for rooms in hotels and guest houses; inquire either at the airport or Europa-Center (see TOURIST INFORMATION OFFICES). The service is free if you write in advance; otherwise a small charge is made. It is always advisable to book well ahead. Berlitz has included a selection of hotels in Berlin in the centre of this guide.

If you would like to stay in a Berliner's home, contact one of the following organizations:

Mitwohnzentrale, Sybelstrasse 53, Berlin 12, tel. 324 30 31

Mitwohnagentur Last Minute, Finowstrasse 8, Berlin 44, tel. 681 50 81

I'd like a single/double room.	**Ich hätte gern ein Einzelzimmer/Doppelzimmer.**
with bath/shower	**mit Bad/Dusche**
What's the rate per night/week?	**Wieviel kostet es pro Nacht/ Woche?**

AIRPORTS. Berlin-Tegel (Otto Lilienthal) lies about 8 km. (5 miles) north-west of the city centre. Taxis and buses circulate between the airport and Bahnhof Zoo. Bus no. 9 leaves from outside the airport arrival hall at intervals averaging 7 $^1/_2$ minutes. The usual flat-rate fare applies. The no. 8 bus serves northern Berlin, terminating at Wilhelmsruh.

After a time as a military airport, Tempelhof (Zentralflughafen) has been reactivated to handle civilian air traffic. It can be reached by U-Bahn line 6 (Platz der Luftbrücke) or bus nos. 4 and 19. A shuttle bus connects Tegel airport with that at Schönefeld, about 19 km. (12 miles) south of the city centre. Schönefeld can be reached by bus no. 36 to the S-Bahn Grünau station.

Airport information: Tegel, tel. 410 11
                                 Tempelhof, tel. 690 91
                                 Schonefeld, tel. 67 20

ALTERNATIVE SCENE. Berlin is a leader in the realm of alternative lifestyle. The best source of information about alternative events in the city is the Informationszentrum,

Hardenbergstrasse 20, Berlin 12, tel. 31 00 40

Most organizations announce meetings and projects in the daily *Tageszeitung*, known familiarly as *taz*, and the magazines *tip*, *zitty* and *tempo*.

BABY-SITTERS. Most hotels will arrange for a sitter to look after your child. It is customary to pay travelling expenses in addition to the fee.

BICYCLE HIRE *(Fahrradverleih)*. Berlin's cyclists are safe from the traffic in their own special network of bicycle lanes, but something of a hazard to pedestrians. You can't beat them so join them. Bikes are easy to rent; call at the Fahrradbüro, Hauptstrasse 146.

BUSES. For city transport, see under TRANSPORT. Long-distance buses serve many destinations in Germany. Coaches depart from the central bus station *(Zentraler Omnibusbahnhof)* near the Funkturm in Messedamm, tel. 301 80 28.

CAMPING. Four major campsites lie on the outskirts of the city in the greener reaches of Berlin:

Zeltplatz in Kladow, Krampnitzer Weg 111, Berlin 22, tel. 365 27 97

Campingplatz Haselhorst, Pulvermühlenweg, Berlin 20, tel. 334 59 55

Campingplatz Dreilinden, Albrechts Teerofen, Berlin 39,
tel. 805 12 01

Intercamping Krossinsee, Werndsdorferstr. 45, Berlin 1186,
tel. 685 86 87

For full information about sites and facilities, consult the guides
published by the German Automobile Club, ADAC, or the Berliner
Camping-Club:

Geisbergstrasse 11, Berlin 30, tel. 24 60 71

CAR HIRE. See also DRIVING. You can arrange to hire a car immediately
upon arrival at Tegel or Schönefeld airports. Otherwise inquire at your
hotel or refer to the yellow pages of the telephone directory under
Autovermietung for addresses of leading firms. To hire a car you'll need
a valid driving licence held for at least one year; the minimum age is 21.
Normally a deposit is charged, but holders of major credit cards are
exempt.

CLIMATE. Berlin's climate follows the continental pattern of cold,
snowy winters and agreeably warm summers with low humidity. If
weather is a consideration, arrange to go in late spring or summer, when
temperatures tend to be mild. You may want to time your visit to coincide
with a special event like the film festival in late February or early March.
Whatever the season, Berlin has a great deal to offer, with a kaleidoscope
of cultural activities (though even Berlin takes a break in July and August)
and a wealth of historical sights.

Average temperatures		J	F	M	A	M	J	J	A	S	O	N	D
°C	max.	2	3	8	13	19	22	25	23	20	13	7	3
°F	min.	−3	−3	0	4	8	12	14	13	10	6	2	−1
°C	max.	35	37	46	56	66	72	75	74	68	56	45	38
°F	min.	26	26	31	39	47	53	57	56	50	42	36	29

Minimum temperatures are measured just before sunrise, maximum temperatures
in the afternoon.

CLOTHING. Pack clothing appropriate to the season: a heavy coat in
winter, lightweight garments and bathing costume in summer, raincoat
and umbrella during the spring and autumn. Dress in Berlin is fairly

casual. High-class hotels and restaurants do, of course, expect a certain standard of attire, but a tie is rarely obligatory.

COMPLAINTS. If something goes wrong that you cannot take care of yourself, report the matter to the Berlin tourist office. In hotels and restaurants, discuss any problems with the proprietor or manager.

CONSULATES *(Konsulat).* Get in touch with the consulate of your home country if something disastrous happens—for example, if you lose your passport, get into trouble with the authorities or the police, or have an accident. The Consul can issue emergency passports, give advice on obtaining money from home, provide a list of lawyers, interpreters and doctors. He cannot pay your bills, lend you money, find you a job or obtain a work permit for you.

Canada	Europa-Center, 1000 Berlin 30, tel. 261 11 61
Eire	Ernst Reuter Platz 10, 1000 Berlin 10, tel. 34 80 08 22
South Africa	Rankestrasse 34, 1000 Berlin 30, tel. 24 15 17
U.K.	Uhlandstrasse 7, 1000 Berlin 12, tel. 309 52 92
U.S.A.	Clayallee 170, 1000 Berlin 33, tel. 819 74 65

CRIME AND THEFT. Compared to most urban centres, Berlin's crime rate is moderate, but it is, unfortunately, on the increase. Take sensible measures, such as leaving your valuables in the hotel safe. Be wary of pickpockets in crowded places, keep your wallet in an inside pocket, and don't leave objects unattended or open to view in a parked car. If you are robbed, report the incident to the hotel receptionist and the nearest police station. The police will provide you with a certificate to present to your insurance company, or to your consulate if your passport has been stolen.

It's a wise precaution to make photocopies of important documents such as passport, plane tickets, and so on, and keep them separately—they may facilitate replacements in case you lose your papers.

I want to report a theft. **Ich möchte einen Diebstahl melden.**

CUSTOMS *(Zoll)* **AND ENTRY FORMALITIES.** There are no restrictions on the import or export of marks or any other Western currency.

For a stay of up to three months, a valid passport is sufficient for citizens of Australia, Canada, New Zealand, South Africa and the U.S.A. Visitors from Eire and the United Kingdom need only an identity card. The chart below shows what you can take into Germany duty-free and, when returning home, into your own country:

Into:		Cigarettes		Cigars		Tobacco	Spirits		Wine
Germany	1)	300	or	75	or	400 g.	1.5 l.	and	5 l.
	2)	200	or	50	or	250 g.	1 l.	or	2 l.
Canada		200	and	50	and	900 g.	1.1 l.	or	1.1 l.
U.K.	3)	200	or	50	or	250 g.	1 l.	and	2 l.
	4)	300	or	75	or	400 g.	1.5 l.	and	5 l.
U.S.A.		200	and	100	or	5)	1 qt.	or	1 qt.

1) Visitors from an E.C. country importing VAT-paid items.
2) Visitors entering from an E.C. country with goods bought duty-free, or visitors from countries outside the E.C.
3) Duty-free items, which can be combined with: 4) duty-paid items.
5) A reasonable quantity.

DRIVING

Entering Germany. To enter Germany with your car you will need:
- a national driving licence (or an international licence for those coming from the U.S.A., Australia and South Africa) car registration papers
- a national identity sticker for your car
- a red warning triangle in case of breakdown
- a first-aid kit

Insurance. Third-party insurance is compulsory. Visitors from abroad, except those from E.C. and certain other European countries, will have to present their international certificate (Green Card) or take out third-party insurance at the border.

Driving conditions. Rush-hour traffic jams and lack of parking space make driving in central Berlin somewhat frustrating. At the beginning and end of peak holiday periods, bottlenecks tend to form on approach roads into Berlin, but outside these times traffic is generally fluid.

Drive on the right, pass on the left. Traffic in Berlin follows the same basic rules that apply in most European cities. Seat belts are obligatory, and that includes back-seat passengers if the car is equipped for them. If you don't wear your seat belt, insurance companies reduce compensation in the event of an accident.

Speed limits. The speed limit is 100 kilometres per hour (62 mph) on all open roads except for motorways and dual carriageways (divided highways), where there's no limit unless otherwise indicated. In town, speed is restricted to 50 kph (31 mph). Cars towing caravans may not exceed 80 kph (50 mph).

Traffic police may confiscate the car keys of persons they consider unfit to drive. Drinking and driving is a very serious offence in Germany. The permissible level of alcohol in the blood is 0.8 per mille (millilitres), the equivalent of about two glasses of beer. Be careful, too, to stay within speed limits; the police are getting more and more strict, and radar is used widely.

Breakdowns. For round-the-clock breakdown service in western Berlin, call 192 11, and in the eastern part of the city 558 88 88.

Fuel and oil *(Benzin; Öl)*. You'll find filling stations everywhere, most of them self-service.

Fluid measures

| imp. gals. 0 | 5 | 10 |
| litres 0 5 10 20 30 40 50 |
| U.S. gals. 0 5 10 |

Distance

| km 0 1 2 3 4 5 6 8 10 12 14 16 |
| miles 0 ½ 1 1½ 2 3 4 5 6 7 8 9 10 |

Road signs. Most road signs used in Berlin are international pictographs, but you might come across some of the following written ones:

Einbahnstrasse	One-way street
Einordnen	Get into lane
Fussgänger	Pedestrians
Kurzparkzone	Short-term parking
Links fahren	Keep left
Parken verboten	No parking
Umleitung	Diversion (Detour)
Vorsicht	Caution

(International) Driving Licence	**(Internationaler) Führerschein**
Car Registration Papers	**Kraftfahrzeugpapiere**
Green Card	**Grüne Karte**
Where's the nearest car park?	**Wo ist der nächste Parkplatz?**
Full tank, please.	**Bitte volltanken.**
Check the oil/tyres/battery, please.	**Kontrollieren Sie bitte das Öl/ die Reifen/die Batterie.**
I've had a breakdown.	**Ich habe eine Panne.**
There's been an accident.	**Es ist ein Unfall passiert.**

ELECTRIC CURRENT. Germany has 220–250 volt, 50-cycle AC. Plugs are the standard continental type, for which British and North American appliances need an adaptor.

EMERGENCIES. See also the relevant section according to the type of emergency.

Emergency telephone numbers:

Police	110	Fire	112
First aid	112 (W), 115 (E)	Ambulance	85 85
Pharmacies	1141 (W), 160 (E)	Drugs	24 70 33
Medical assistance	31 00 31 (W), 12 59 (E)		

Could you place an emergency call for me to the…?	**Würden Sie bitte … für mich anrufen?**
police/fire brigade/hospital	**die Polizei/die Feuerwehr/ das Krankenhaus**

GETTING TO BERLIN

By air
There are direct daily flights to Berlin from major airports all over the world. The cheapest fares on regular flights are APEX, which must be booked and paid for three to four weeks in advance. However, if you want a more flexible ticket, you should discuss your plans carefully with a reliable travel agent who will advise you on the best deals. Some carriers have a special round-trip fare that can be ticketed at any time. Unless you

leave things until the last minute, you will probably be able to book a charter flight or package including a hotel room, generally at rates and conditions even more reasonable than APEX.

By rail

See also TRAINS. Two trains depart from London for Berlin daily: from Victoria via Dover and Ostend or from Liverpool Street station by way of Harwich and the Hook of Holland. You might have to change trains in Hanover.

First-class travel on the Bundesbahn costs double the second-class fare. A supplement is charged for travel on EuroCity and InterCity trains. Children under 4 travel free in Germany, those 4 to 12 pay half fare. There are two "saver" tickets, the fixed-price return *Sparpreis*, valid for one month, and the even cheaper *Super-Sparpreis*, valid for 10 days. If you are travelling with someone else, you can combine the saver ticket with the *Mitfahrer-Fahrpreis*, which applies for distances over 203 km. The first person pays full or saver fare, the others each pay half. Families, seniors and young people pay half fare with ID-cards valid for one year. These are obtainable at railway stations.

There are also several "go-as-you-please" passes. The Eurailpass allows unlimited travel on trains in 17 European countries including Germany, and certain ferries. It is sold only to those residing outside Europe and North Africa. European residents under 26 can buy an Inter-Rail card, valid in most European countries. It is issued for one month and enables a 50 per cent reduction on train tickets in the country of purchase and on ferries, and unlimited free travel elsewhere. The Deutsche Bundesbahn also issues a tourist card, the GermanRail pass, sold only to visitors. Valid for 4, 9 or 16 days, it permits unlimited travel on trains and DB Touring buses. You can buy it in Germany at major railway stations and airports, and overseas at GermanRail offices.

By road

The Harwich/Hamburg crossing takes 21 hours and brings you closer to Berlin (300 km., 186 miles) than other Channel ports.

GUIDES and TOURS. The tourist office will put you in touch with qualified guides and interpreters if you want a personally conducted tour or need linguistic assistance.

City sightseeing tours by bus provide an excellent introduction to Berlin. Before you join the tour that includes the Pergamon Museum, make sure it is given in English as well as German. Daily excursions by coach to Potsdam are also available, as well as weekend trips to other places in Germany, including Dresden and Wittenberg. There are several companies that specialize in boat trips, too. During the summer season, BVG, Berlin's public transport company, offers sightseeing tours in historical double-decker buses, departing from Breitscheidplatz at Kaiser-Wilhelm-Gedächtniskirche.

Most sightseeing tours depart from the Kurfürstendamm, between Rankestrasse and Fasanenstrasse, or Unter den Linden:

Severin & Kühn Berliner Stadtrundfahrt, tel. 883 10 15. Departure points: Ku'damm 216, between Uhlandstrasse and Fasanenstrasse; Unter den Linden/Staatsoper.

Berolina, tel. 882 20 91. Departure points: Ku'damm at Meinekestrasse; Unter den Linden, corner Universitätstrasse; or Palasthotel.

Berliner Bären-Stadtrundfahrt, tel. 213 40 77. Departure points: Ku'damm at Rankestrasse, opposite Kaiser-Wilhelm-Gedächtniskirche.

BVB, tel. 882 68 47. Departure points: Ku'damm 225, at Joachimstaler Strasse (a combined bus-boat trip); Unter den Linden, corner of Friedrichstrasse at the Lindenkorso.

Europäisches Reisebüro Berlin-Tourist: 3-hour sightseeing tours from Hauptbahnhof or Haus des Reisens (Alexanderplatz).

HEALTH and MEDICAL CARE. Ask your insurance company before leaving home if you are covered for medical treatment in Germany. Visitors who are not reimbursed for medical bills abroad can take out a short-term holiday policy before setting out. Citizens of E.C. countries may use the German Health Services for medical treatment. Ask for the requisite form at your local Health and Social Security Office.

In the event of accident or serious illness, call for an ambulance, tel. 85 85, or ask the medical emergency service, tel. 31 00 31 (W), 12 59 (E), to recommend a competent doctor. You can also contact the American or British consulates for a list of English-speaking doctors and dentists.

Pharmacies are open during normal shopping hours. At night and on Sundays and holidays, all chemists display the address of the nearest one open. For emergencies, call 1141 (W), 160 (E). Condoms *(Präservative)* can be bought in pharmacies and drugstores.

Where's the nearest (all-night) pharmacy?	**Wo ist die nächste (Dienst-) Apotheke?**
I need a doctor/dentist.	**Ich brauche einen Arzt/Zahnarzt.**

HEALTH FOODS. Germans are very much aware of the trend for healthy eating, and vegetarians are especially well catered for. You'll have no problem finding a *Vegetarische Restaurant* serving *Vollwert-Küche* (whole foods). Health foods are sold in shops known as *Bioladen*, and most supermarkets also have a health food section.

Do you have vegetarian dishes?	**Haben Sie vegetarische Gerichte?**

HOURS

Museums generally open from 9 a.m. to 5 p.m., closing days are usually Monday or Friday. To be on the safe side, check at the tourist office before you go.

Restaurants. Breakfast is served until 10 a.m., lunch from noon to 2 p.m. and dinner from 6 to 9.30 p.m.

Shops are generally open from 9 a.m. to 6 p.m., Monday to Friday, till 1 or 2 p.m. on Saturdays (until 6 p.m. on the first Saturday of the month), and 8.30 p.m. on Thursdays.

Tourist information offices. The Europa-Center office opens daily from 7.30 a.m. to 10.30 p.m., while the Tegel Airport office operates from 8 a.m. to 10.30 p.m. The Informationszentrum answers queries from 8 a.m. to 7 p.m., Monday to Friday, 8 a.m. to 4 p.m. Saturday, but the administration office can be contacted only from 9 a.m. to 3 p.m., Monday to Friday. For additional information, contact the Informationszentrum am Alexanderplatz/Fernsehturm, tel. 212 46 75, from 8 a.m. to 8 p.m.

LANGUAGE. There is a Berlin dialect, but most people you'll meet will speak *Hochdeutsch*—normal German. As Germans are great linguists, you'll probably be able to manage with just English, which is widely understood.

When greeting people, it's customary to say *Guten Tag* (good day), and when taking leave, *Auf Wiedersehen* (goodbye); the less formal *Tschüss*, meaning "Bye" or "See you soon", is a privilege of friends. When taking leave of someone on the telephone, you should say *Auf Wiederhören*, literally, "Until we hear each other again".

The Berlitz phrase book GERMAN FOR TRAVELLERS covers most of the situations you are likely to encounter in Germany, and the German-English/English-German pocket dictionary contains a special menu-reader supplement.

Do you speak English?	**Sprechen Sie Englisch?**

LAUNDRY AND DRY-CLEANING. Having your laundry washed or cleaned by the hotel is the quickest and most convenient method, but prices are correspondingly high. It is therefore worth seeking out a *Waschsalon* (launderette) or *Wäscherei* (laundry). Dry-cleaning usually takes two days. Some cleaners offer a quick service *(Schnellreinigung)* which takes a minimum of two hours and is slightly more expensive.

LOST PROPERTY. Western Berlin's general lost-property office *(Fundbüro der Polizei)* is at Platz der Luftbrücke 6, Berlin 42, tel. 699 17. In eastern Berlin, the general office is situated at Wilhelm-Pieck-Strasse 164, tel. 282 34 72. But if you know where you left your property behind, the best thing to do is call the *Fundbüro* of the service concerned. If it was on the public transport in western Berlin, contact the BVG at Potsdamer Strasse 184, tel. 216 14 13. For the eastern Berlin S-Bahn, inquire at the S-Bahnhof Marx-Engels-Platz, tel. 492 16 71, or the *Fundsammelstelle* in the U-Bahnhof Alexanderplatz. Articles are kept here one day, then sent to the general office on the next working day.

For anything lost in a post office or telephone call box, inquire at the main post office, Bahnhof Zoo, tel. 313 97 99, and if you leave something in a taxi, call the company (see numbers below under TAXIS).

I've lost my wallet/my bag/ my passport.	**Ich habe meine Brieftasche/ meine Tasche/meinen Pass verloren.**

MAIL. Berlin's central post office *(Postamt)* is located in Bahnhof Zoo. It stays open 24 hours a day and handles mail, telegrams, public telex and telephone services. You can have mail directed to you here, c/o

> Hauptpostlagernd
> Postamt 120
> Bahnhof Zoo
> D-1000 Berlin 12

Take your passport or identity card when you go to collect your mail.

The post office at Tegel Airport is open daily from 6.30 a.m. to 9 p.m. Other branch offices of Germany's Bundespost generally open Monday to Friday from 8 a.m. to 6 or 6.30 p.m., and until noon on Saturdays.

In the eastern part of the city, the main post office, Postamt Berlin 17, Strasse der Pariser Kommune 8–10, is open 24 hours a day. The most

convenient branch offices in this area are at the Friedrichstrasse railway
station and Alexanderplatz S-Bahn station.

Faxes can be sent from public "copy centres".

A stamp for this letter/postcard, please.	**Eine Briefmarke für diesen Brief/diese Karte, bitte.**
express (special delivery)	**Eilzustellung**
airmail	**Luftpost**
registered	**Einschreiben**
Have you received any mail for …?	**Ist Post da für …?**

MAPS. Even Berliners need maps to get around their city. Excellent free
maps are available at the tourist offices, most banks, car-hire firms and
bigger hotels. The maps in this book were designed by Falk-Verlag,
Hamburg.

I'd like a street map of Berlin	**Ich möchte einen Stadtplan von Berlin.**

MEETING PEOPLE. Berlin is a marvellous place for making friends.
Life is essentially "outdoors", on café terraces and in bars (notably around
Ku'damm, Kantstrasse and Savignyplatz), and everyone is very sociable.
If there's a seat free at your table, you can be sure someone will come and
sit in it and strike up a conversation.

MONEY MATTERS

Currency. Germany's monetary unit is the *Deutsche Mark (DM)*. The mark
is divided into 100 *Pfennig (Pf.)*.
Coins: 1, 2, 5, 10 and 50 Pf. and DM 1, 2 and 5.
Notes: DM 5, 10, 20, 50, 100, 200, 500 and 1,000.

Banking hours are usually from 9 a.m. to 1 p.m. Monday to Friday. Most
banks remain open two afternoons a week (often Tuesday and Thursday
from 3.30 to 6 p.m.); however days and times vary, so you'll have to check
posted notices. Branches in the big stores operate during normal shopping
hours. Currency can be changed at offices in Bahnhof Zoo from 8 a.m. to
9 p.m. Monday to Saturday, 10 a.m. to 6 p.m. on Sunday and holidays, and
in Europa-Center from 9 a.m. to 6 p.m. Monday to Friday, 9 a.m. to 4 p.m.
Saturday.

Changing money. Foreign currency can be changed at ordinary banks *(Bank)*, savings banks *(Sparkasse)* and currency exchange offices *(Wechselstube)*. Hotels, travel agencies and Berlin's central post office also have exchange facilities, but rates are less favourable. The same is true of currency and traveller's cheques changed in shops or restaurants.

Credit cards, traveller's cheques, eurocheques. These are accepted in most hotels, restaurants and big shops.

I want to change some pounds/ dollars.	**Ich möchte Pfund/ Dollars wechseln.**
Do you accept traveller's cheques?	**Nehmen Sie Reiseschecks?**
Can I pay with this credit card?	**Kann ich mit dieser Kreditkarte zahlen?**

NEWSPAPERS and MAGAZINES *(Zeitung; Zeitschrift).* Major American, British and other European newspapers and magazines are on sale at newsagents and kiosks in the city centre, as well as at big hotels and at the airports. You'll also find the *International Herald Tribune,* published in Paris. The kiosk around the corner from Bahnhof Zoo has one of the best selections of foreign periodicals in town.

PHOTOGRAPHY. Some of the world's best cameras come from Germany, so you might well consider getting equipped here. All makes of film are easily found and can be developed overnight or even within an hour if need be. Airport security machines use X-rays which can fog your film after more than four scannings. To be safe, ask the officer to check it by hand, or enclose it in a special X-ray-proof bag.

I'd like a roll of film for this camera.	**Ich hätte gern einen Film für diesen Apparat.**
Can you develop this film for tomorrow?	**Können Sie diesen Film bis morgen entwickeln?**
black-and-white film	**Schwarzweissfilm**
colour prints	**Farbfilm**
colour slides	**Diafilm**

PLANNING YOUR BUDGET. The following list will give you some idea of what prices to expect in Berlin. But as we can never keep up with inflation, they can only be considered approximate.

Airport transfer. City bus to Bahnhof Zoo DM 2.70, taxi DM 25.

Baby-sitters. DM 15–20 per hour.

Camping. DM 18 for two persons with car or caravan (trailer).

Car hire. *VW Polo* DM 70 per day, DM 0.70 per km., DM 150 per weekend (Friday noon–Monday 9 a.m.) up to 1,500 km. free, DM 700 per week with unlimited mileage.

Entertainment. Cinema DM 12–15 (DM 6 on Wednesdays), club cinema/foreign films DM 9–11, theatre DM 15–60, discotheque DM 20–50, nightclub DM 25–200.

Hairdressers. *Man's* haircut DM 15–35. *Woman's* haircut DM 30–60, shampoo and set DM 20–45, blow-dry DM 25–45.

Hotels (double room per night). Luxury class DM 265–475, first class DM 195–300, medium range DM 140–205, budget class DM 80–115. *Guest house* DM 60–120.

Meals and drinks Breakfast DM 6–15, lunch or dinner in fairly good establishment DM 20–40, bottle of wine (German) DM 25–40, beer (small bottle) DM 3.50–6, soft drink (small bottle) DM 3–5, coffee DM 2.50–4.

Museums. DM 3–6 (often free).

Public transport. BVG: single ticket DM 2.70, children DM 1.70; *Sammelkarte* DM 9.20, children DM 5.60; Berlin Ticket (valid for 24 hours from start of first journey) DM 9, children DM 5.

Shopping bag. 1 kilo of bread DM 4–6, 250 g. butter DM 2–2.60, 100 g. German sausage DM 1.60–2.50, 100 g. smoked ham DM 2.60–3, 100 g. meat or vegetable salad DM 1.60–4, 100 g. cheese DM 1.80–3, beer ($^1/_2$ litre) DM 1.

Sightseeing. East/West City Tour ($2^1/2$ hours) DM 30, Big Berlin Tour (3 hours) DM 38, Potsdam tour (4 hours) DM 49.

Taxis. Initial charge DM 3.40.

POLICE (*Polizei*). Germany's police wear green uniforms. You'll see them on white motorcycles or in green-and-white cars. The police emergency number is 110. Berlin's central police station *(Polizeipräsidium)* is at Platz der Luftbrücke 6, Berlin 42.

Where's the nearest police station? **Wo ist die nächste Polizeiwache?**

PUBLIC HOLIDAYS *(Feiertag)*. The chart below shows the public holidays celebrated in Berlin, when shops, banks, official departments and many restaurants are closed. If a holidays falls on a Thursday, many people take the Friday off too, to make a long weekend.

On December 24 (Christmas Eve), shops stay open till midday, but most restaurants, theatres, cinemas and concert halls are closed.

Jan 1	*Neujahr*	New Year's Day
May 1	*Tag der Arbeit*	Labour Day
June 17	*Tag der deutschen Einheit*	Day of National Unity
Dec. 25, 26	*Weihnachten*	Christmas
Movable dates:	*Karfreitag*	Good Friday
	Ostermontag	Easter Monday
	Christi Himmelfahrt	Ascension Day
	Pfingstmontag	Whit Monday
	Buss- und Bettag	Day of Prayer and Repentance (3rd Wed. in November)

RADIO AND TV *(Radio, Fernsehen)*. You can easily pick up the BBC World Service, American Forces Network (AFN) or the Voice of America. Shortwave reception is excellent, especially at night. As for television, there are two national channels—ARD and ZDF, plus a regional station. Most hotels can also receive satellite channels from Great Britain and the U.S.A.

RESTAURANTS. See also p. 93, and the list of recommended establishments inserted in the centre of this guide.

Most restaurants display a menu *(Speisekarte)* outside. Besides the à la carte menu, there are usually one or more set menus *(Menü* or *Gedeck)*. Value-added tax *(MwSt)* and the service charge *(Bedienung)* are usually included. Appetizers (or starters) are listed on the menu under *Vorspeisen, Kleine Gerichte* or *Kalte Platten.* Soups *(Suppen)* and stews *(Eintopfgerichte)* can be very hearty and sometimes enough for a whole meal. Fish and seafood come under *Fisch und Meeresfrüchte,* meat is *Fleisch.* Vegetables *(Gemüse)* served with the main dish are referred to as the *Beilage,* which can be simply potatoes, or sometimes rice or pasta or several green vegetables. Cheese is *Käse,* fruit *Obst,* and dessert is

Nachtisch, Nachspeise or *Süssspeise*. Note that the word *Art* means "style", so *Griesspudding nach Grossmutters Art* is semolina pudding the way Granny made it. We have listed below a few basic terms to help you understand the menu, but remember that in German words are often strung together and you will have to do some detective work. For example, *Kalbsbrust* means breast of veal, *Erdbeereis* strawberry ice cream.

To help you order...

Waiter/Waitress!	**Herr Ober/Fräulein, bitte!**
May I have the menu, please?	**Kann ich bitte die Speisekarte haben?**
What do you recommend?	**Was würden Sie mir empfehlen?**
I'd like a/an/some ...	**Ich hätte gern ...**

bread	**Brot**	mustard	**Senf/Mostrich**
butter	**Butter**	pepper	**Pfeffer**
coffee	**Kaffee**	potatoes	**Kartoffeln**
cream	**Sahne**	salad	**Salat**
ice cream	**Eis**	salt	**Salz**
lemon	**Zitrone**	sugar	**Zucker**
milk	**Milch**	tea	**Tee**
mineral water	**Mineralwasser**	wine	**Wein**

... and read the menu

Aal	eel	**Huhn**	chicken
Apfel	apple	**Hummer**	lobster
Apfelsine	orange	**Kalbfleisch**	veal
Auflauf	soufflé	**Kaninchen**	rabbit
Austern	oysters	**Kartoffeln**	potatoes
Blumenkohl	cauliflower	**Kohl**	cabbage
Bohnen	beans	**Krabben**	shrimp
Dorsch	cod	**Krebs**	crayfish
Ente	duck	**Kuchen**	cake
Erbsen	peas	**Kutteln**	tripe
Erdbeeren	strawberries	**Lachs**	salmon
Fasan	pheasant	**Lammfleisch**	lamb
Forelle	trout	**Leber**	liver
Gans	goose	**Muscheln**	mussels
Hammelfleisch	mutton	**Nieren**	kidneys
Hase	hare	**Pilze**	mushrooms
Himbeeren	raspberries	**Pommes frites**	chips (French fries)

Pfirsich	peach	**Schweinefleisch**	pork
Reis	rice	**Seezunge**	sole
Reh	venison	**Speck**	bacon
Rindfleisch	beef	**Steinbutt**	turbot
Rosenkohl	brussels sprouts	**Truthahn**	turkey
Sardellen	anchovies	**Wildschwein**	boar
Schinken	ham	**Wurst**	sausage
Schnecken	snails	**Zwiebeln**	onions

SMOKING. Foreign brands of cigarettes *(Zigaretten)*, manufactured under German licence, are sold in specialized tobacco shops *(Tabakwarenladen)*, at kiosks and from vending machines. Most of the domestic makes resemble American cigarettes. As a rule, smoking is prohibited in theatres, cinemas, buses and trams. Trains have special smoking compartments. Smoking is less and less appreciated in public areas and there are non-smoking areas in restaurants; respect the signs, which may be the international pictograph of a crossed-out cigarette, or the words *Nicht rauchen*.

TAXIS. Berlin taxis are mostly beige in colour. Catch one at a rank, at busy locations such as the Ku'damm/Joachimstaler Strasse intersection, or hail a driver cruising the street. You can also book in advance through your hotel receptionist or by phoning direct to one of the following numbers: 69 02 (W), 26 10 26 (W), 24 00 24 (W), 24 02 02 (W), 33 66 (E), 36 44 (E).

TELEPHONE. The sign on phone booths indicates whether the phone can be used for national or international calls: a yellow square with black receiver means national calls only, while a green square means that national and international calls are possible. Area code numbers are listed in a special directory. The use of phone cards *(Telefonkarte)* is widespread; they can be obtained at any post office. Communications within Germany and to neighbouring countries are cheaper from 6 p.m. to 8 a.m. weekdays and all day Saturday and Sunday. Rates for Canada and the United States are reduced from midnight to noon. Calls placed by hotels and restaurants generally carry a considerable surcharge.

Some useful numbers:

Inquiries: domestic 1188, international 001 18
Operator: domestic 010, international 0010

Until the telecommunications system is restructured, western Berlin is considered long-distance from the eastern part of the city, and to get through from East to West you'll have to dial 849 first; in the other direction the area code is 9.

Can I use the telephone?	**Kann ich das Telefon benutzen?**
Can you get me this number in ...	**Können Sie mich mit dieser Nummer in ... verbinden?**
reverse-charge (collect) call	**R-Gespräch**
personal (person-to-person) call	**Gespräch mit Voranmeldung**

TIME DIFFERENCES. Germany follows Central European Time (GMT + 2):

New York	London	**Berlin**	Jo'burg	Sydney	Auckland
6 a.m.	11 a.m.	**noon**	noon	8 p.m.	10 p.m.

TIPPING. Since a service charge is normally included in hotel and restaurant bills, tipping is not obligatory. However it's appropriate to give something extra to porters, cloakroom attendants and so on for their services. The chart below makes some suggestions as to how much to leave.

Hairdresser/barber	10–15%
Lavatory attendant	DM 0.50–1
Maid, per week	DM 5-10
Porter, per bag	DM 1–2
Taxi driver	round off
Tourist guide	DM 1-2
Waiter	(optional) 5%

TOILETS. Public toilets are readily found. If there's an attendant, and handtowels and soap are offered, you should leave a small tip. Always have 10-Pfennig coins ready in case the door has a slot machine.

Toilets may be labelled with symbols of a man or a woman or the initials W.C. Otherwise *Herren* (Gentlemen) or *Damen* (Ladies) are indicated.

Where are the toilets, please?   **Wo sind die Toiletten, bitte?**

TOURIST INFORMATION OFFICES. The German National Tourist Board—Deutsche Zentrale für Tourismus e.V. (DZT)—can inform you about when to go, where to stay and what to see in Berlin. The headquarters is at:

Beethovenstrasse 69, D-6000 Frankfurt am Main, tel. 757 20.

The national tourist organization also maintains offices in many countries throughout the world:

Canada	P.O. Box 417, 2 Fundy, Place Bonaventure, Montreal, Que. H5A 1B8; tel. (514) 878 98 85
	1290 Bay Street, Toronto, Ontario M5R 2C3; tel. (416) 968 15 70
United Kingdom	61 Conduit Street, London W1R 0EN; tel. (071) 734 26 00
U.S.A.	747 Third Avenue, New York, NY 10017; tel. (212) 308 33 00
	Broadway Plaza, Suite 2230, 444 South Flower Street, Los Angeles, CA 90071; tel. (213) 688 73 32. Or dial the toll-free reservation and information service: 1 800 237 54 69

Berlin's tourist offices are situated in the arrival hall of Tegel airport, tel. 41 01 31 45; at Bahnhof Zoo, tel. 313 90 63; on the motorway south-west of the city at Dreilinden, tel. 803 90 57; and at Alexanderplatz (TV-Tower), tel. 212 46 75. The main office is in Europa-Center (entrance in Budapester Strasse). Address inquiries to:

Verkehrsamt Berlin, Europa-Center, 1000 Berlin 30, tel. 262 60 31.

In addition to providing free maps, lists and brochures, Berlin's tourist offices offer a hotel booking service. The official *Berlin Programm* of events (concerts, theatre, exhibitions) is also on sale there.

The Informationszentrum (see under ALTERNATIVE SCENE) organizes special-interest programmes and educational visits for groups of young people.

TRAINS. See also GETTING TO BERLIN. In western Germany, Deutsche Bundesbahn (DB) trains are extremely comfortable and fast, as well as punctual. The transit railway lines between western Germany and Berlin, however, are still operated by the Deutsche Reichbahn. Since unification, you can get off either at western Berlin's main station, Bahnhof Zoo, or continue to Friedrichstrasse or Hauptbahnhof in the eastern part of the city (if that is your destination) without having to change trains.

TRANSPORT. Berlin is served by an efficient network of buses, trams, U-Bahn (underground railway) and S-Bahn (suburban railway) administered by the Berliner Verkehrs-Betriebe or BVG, the BVB and the DR. The U-Bahn comprises eight lines covering the inner city and many outlying districts, while the bus service reaches virtually every corner of Berlin. Special express buses bearing a triangle symbol shuttle between Bahnhof Zoo and the Grunewald, Pfaueninsel and (in summer) various beaches.

The U-Bahn operates from 4 a.m. to about midnight or 1 a.m. (1 to 2 a.m. on Sunday). Buses run round the clock, though the skeleton night services are less frequent. The last U-Bahn train departs from Friedrichstrasse station for western Berlin at 2 a.m.

The M-Bahn (magnetically levitated train), a pioneer transport system, runs smoothly between Gleisdreieck U-Bahn station and the Kulturforum in the Tiergarten area.

Tickets are interchangeable between trains and buses, entitling you to free transfers for up to 90 minutes so long as you travel in the same direction. Have plenty of small change on you as tickets are distributed in vending machines at the U-Bahn stations and most bus stops. If the machine rejects a coin (they tend to be unpredictable), try with another. Stamp your ticket in one of the red machines on station platforms and in buses. To buy a ticket on the bus itself, have the exact change ready. You can also buy a ticket valid for four rides *(Sammelkarte)*, or the 24-hour Berlin Ticket which can be used on all BVG and BVB lines without restriction, including certain ferries. Groups of six or more may apply for a group ticket *(Sonderwochenkarte)* good for seven days of group and individual transport on BVG and BVB vehicles. A discount is made for children under 14.

One-day tourist cards save a lot of hassle; they are available at Friedrichstrasse station and are valid for all forms of public transport.

WATER. Tap water is perfectly safe to drink; only rarely will you see the warning *Kein Trinkwasser* (not suitable for drinking).

YOUTH HOSTELS. For full information about hostels in the city, contact the local section of the German Youth Hostel Association (Deutsches Jugendherbergswerk - DJH):

Tempelhofer Ufer 32, 1000 Berlin 61, tel. 262 30 24

SOME USEFUL EXPRESSIONS

yes/no	**ja/nein**
please/thank you	**bitte/danke**
excuse me/you're welcome	**Entschuldigung/gern geschehen**
how long/how far	**wie lange/wie weit**
where/when/how	**wo/wann/wie**
yesterday/today/tomorrow	**gestern/heute/morgen**
day/week/month/year	**Tag/Woche/Monat/Jahr**
left/right	**links/rechts**
big/small	**gross/klein**
cheap/expensive	**billig/teuer**
hot/cold	**heiss/kalt**
open/closed	**offen/geschlossen**
free (vacant)/occupied	**frei/besetzt**
I don't understand	**Ich verstehe nicht.**
What does this mean?	**Was bedeutet das?**

NUMBERS

0	**null**	16	**sechzehn**
1	**eins**	17	**siebzehn**
2	**zwei**	18	**achtzehn**
3	**drei**	19	**neunzehn**
4	**vier**	20	**zwanzig**
5	**fünf**	21	**einundzwanzig**
6	**sechs**	30	**dreissig**
7	**sieben**	40	**vierzig**
8	**acht**	50	**fünfzig**
9	**neun**	60	**sechzig**
10	**zehn**	70	**siebzig**
11	**elf**	80	**achtzig**
12	**zwölf**	90	**neunzig**
13	**dreizehn**	100	**(ein)hundert**
14	**vierzehn**	101	**hunderteins**
15	**fünfzehn**	1000	**(ein)tausend**

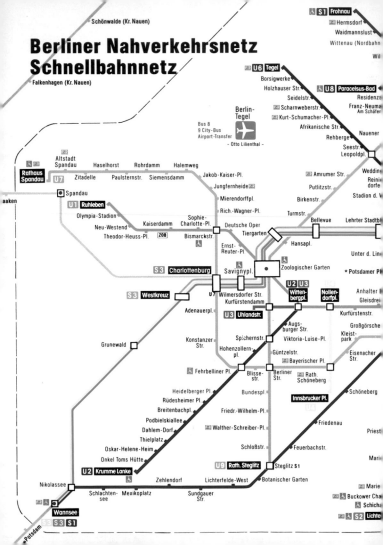

Berliner Nahverkehrsnetz
Schnellbahnnetz

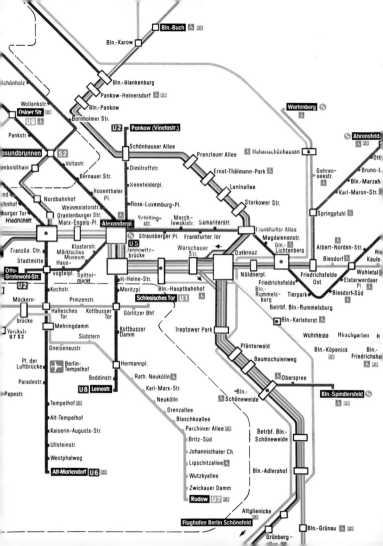

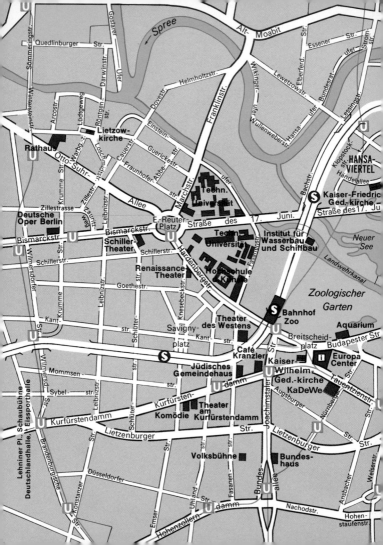

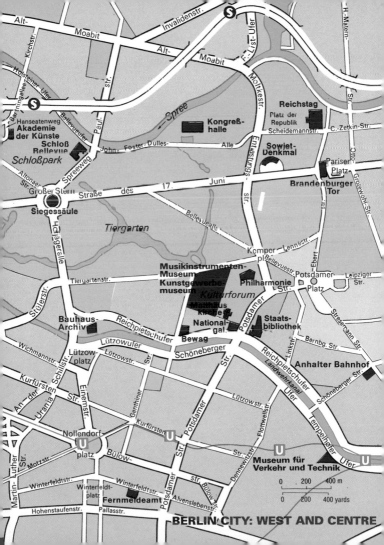

BERLIN CITY: WEST AND CENTRE

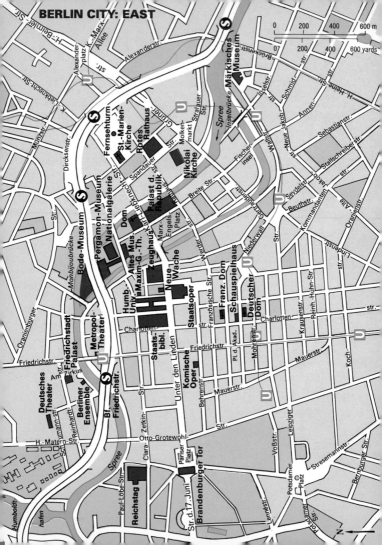

INDEX

An asterisk (*) next to a page number indicates a map reference. Where there is more than one set of references, the one in **bold type** refers to the main entry.